# Advance Praise

"What captured me most in reading Dr. Oster's insightful and authentic exploration of how one might brand one's gifts and strengths in her/his pursuit of a life of meaning and income is the enormous range of disciplines she taps to convey a vast web of enchantments: literature, mythology, fairy tales, stories, theories of psychology, Eastern meditation practices—the list goes on.

Underneath it all is a red thread of certainty: that the human imagination is boundless, ever-active, energetically intense and often unconscious in a person's daily life. Her book is a mythically-inflected, beautifully ordered and coherent response to such sleepiness. I especially found her writing prompts to awaken the soul, most original and engaging."

**DENNIS PATRICK SLATTERY, PH.D**
author of *Bridge Work: Essays on Mythology, Literature and Psychology*

"Kris's teachings are like orgasmic vitamins for your soul. In *Return to Enchantment*, Kris teaches you how to weave mythical archetypes to create a truly arresting brand. This book is radically different than the often stale & recycled business/brand books on the market. I can barely wait to witness the creative bursts and utterly pleasurable brands birthed from *Return to Enchantment*. Warning: this book is highly addictive!"

**MELISSA CASSERA**
www.melissacassera.com

"Ideas and energy sparkle and pop, spangled like diamond-bright drops from the mermaid's tail in Kris Oster's new book, *Return to Enchantment*. Forgo your darkest fantasies of becoming the next Willy Loman as you work to bring your venture to life, buoyed by the possibility and lightness that Kris offers while you are emboldened by the deep dives she makes into the infinite depths of imagination. Delightful, genuinely enchanting, and beyond all, generous."

**LEIGH MELANDER, PH.D**
www.spillian.com

"Reading the introduction to *Return to Enchantment* felt a long-awaited, deep sigh of relief. As a classic first-born-type A-overachiever type, whose addiction to 'doing' typically overshadows a desire for 'being'… this book is the answer to my prayer. I have been hearing among my entrepreneur colleagues and within my own heart, a desire for creating abundant livelihood while simultaneously living a spiritually awake, self-care infused and magical life. These have been our questions: "How might I be successful and deeply fulfilled? Is it possible to achieve without sacrificing time, freedom, connection? I want to experience magic with my children, my partner, and in my work, but who has that?" Finally, (thank you Kris Oster!) appears the blueprint for self-discovery and success that is resonantly personal, nothing short of miraculous, and absolutely available."

**MADDY VERTENTEN**
www.maddyv.com

"*Return to Enchantment* is a deliciously juicy and totally necessary business resource that no other you would have experienced on the 'business development shelves of your local bookstore.

It will show you how to work with mythical archetypes to create a true-to-you brand. I didn't even wait 'til I'd finished the book before I started implementing what is being shared in these pages, it's too good! Kris has a beautiful way of making this ancient wisdom totally on-point for women who are creating businesses in the 21st century. I love Kris, I love this book."

**LISA LISTER**
author of *Code Red: Know Your Flow, Unlock Your Super Powers + Create a Bloody Amazing Life*

## *Return to Enchantment* **Resources**

Looking for some additional support along the way? We've put together a collection of companion audio meditations, bonus material and worksheets.

Head to **returntoenchantment.com** to download them now!

Minette,

wishing you an
eternity of luscious
marketing!

Many blessings,

Kris

# Return to Enchantment

*Your Guide to Creating a Magical Livelihood*

Kris Oster, Ph.D

ISBN: 978-1-938397-99-8

Published by Enchanted Entrepreneurs Press, Santa Barbara

Edited by Nancy Oster
Cover by Angie Mroczka
Typeset by Angie Mroczka

Printed in the United States of America

# Contents

# Introduction

## A Prelude...

*Let us remember that the most valuable resource in our business is not our clients or our brilliant ideas... it is ourselves. Pure, naked.*

*I invite you to enter the temple of desires + dreams. Wishes. Longings. Sadness. Joy. Empty spaces waiting to be filled.*

*In deep reverence bow to your Soul, your mirror self in the Otherworlds, who knows you so intimately. No secrets to hide.*

*Share your intentions with your Soul as you engage with this book. You'll be spending much more time together. Celebrating. Worshipping.*

## Welcome Magical Being!

Just knowing you're here with me to do this work NOW melts my heart open. I'm so grateful.

I felt the calling to write *Return to Enchantment* because much of the material in books and courses for entrepreneurs is trendy or ephemeral. I write to lend my art and my ideas to what I hope will be a far-reaching perspective that lives beyond me or you. The ancient myths, stories and fairytales from cultures all around the world are all alive within us. They breathe vibrantly through our brands as Inanna, Demeter, Dionysus, Psyche, Snow White and Yemaya.

Psychologist CG Jung was well aware of the magical function of the imagination. In his writings about the connections between psychology and alchemy, Jung equates *essence* or *quintessence* with the imaginative faculties: "Imagination is therefore a concentrated extract of the life forces, both physical and psychic…"

While thinking about the primacy of imagination in my world, my daughter Saraphina's innocent and engaging stories came to mind immediately. She has a deep inner knowing that she can be anything, or anyone, she wants to be.

As you work with your imagination now, as an adult, connect with your childhood dreams. What were your favorite stories? Enjoy games that you played over and over. Go back to the inner child within your heart. The operative word here is PLAY.

The imaginative faculty belongs to the heart.

What the eyes can't see and the brain can't wrap its head around, the heart knows to be true and real.

One thing I've heard nearly all of my clients say is that they wish the world was *really* magical like that of Harry Potter or Narnia or Snow White.

This perplexed me because I see magic and miracles happening around me all of the time—they are natural, everyday occurrences. We just don't notice them.

One of the best definitions of magic comes straight from 20th century occultist Dion Fortune: "Magic is the art of causing changes to take place in consciousness in accordance with will."

Magic has more to do with perception than concretization of thought, e.g., wave your magic wand and turn your ex-lover into a toad. Magic is imaginative, but not *imaginary*.

*Return to Enchantment* will help you become conscious of the archetypes in your imaginative psyche that live through you and your brand. You will begin to choose images, both textual and visual, that resonate most for you and your audience.

Using images and words based on the archetypal themes from our most beloved myths, helps our audiences tap into their own yearning to create something eternal.

Whether we are writing marketing copy for a sales page or writing a memoir, we can choose words and images that vibrate with the essence of an archetype to create something healing, beautiful and memorable. The magical essences carried by the stories and archetypes we use invite others into these mystical and enchanted spaces.

In essence, you are conjuring your own brand of sacred magic.

The central idea of my work is to bring spiritual and archetypal energies into the physical realm through our businesses and brands. The objective: bringing Heaven to Earth.

**Incarnate your brand.**

# What is an archetype?

*"By setting up a universe which tends to hold everything we do, see, and say in the sway of its cosmos, an archetype is best comparable with a God."*

**–James Hillman**

Jung defines his collective unconscious as "[…] factors and motifs that arrange the psychic elements into certain images […] in such a way that they can be recognized only from the effects they produce." (*CW* 11:222).

An archetype contains mythological motifs or images that function on an invisible, unconscious level. Cultural and personal experiences transform archetypal ideas and images into external phenomena.

> All the most powerful ideas in history go back to archetypes. This is particularly true of religious ideas, but the central concepts of science, philosophy, and ethics are no exception to this rule. In their present form they are variants of archetypal ideas, created by consciously applying and adapting these ideas to reality. For it is the function of consciousness not only to recognize and assimilate the external world through the gateway of the senses, but to translate into visible reality the world within us. (Jung, *CW* 8:342)

Archetypes are an invitation into possibility, they are not set in stone. They are the spark of a conversation, not the end of the line. Think of an archetype as the blueprint or skeletal structure that supports your diverse and beautiful outer persona.

Stereotypes are not archetypes. A stereotype is not a sustaining, life-giving image. It's stuck and concretized. Stereotypes are oversimplified and exaggerated images that have no healing potential or depth.

For example, if you say "I am Aphrodite" and feel a surge of delight in your own sensuality you invite that archetype to infuse your being.

However a woman who acts and dresses like a sex kitten and is called a "slut" is caught in a stereotype, especially if she believes them.

From the archetypal psychological perspective, (a branch of depth psychology founded by James Hillman), each mythological figure represents a piece of the human psyche: for example, Yemaya is known as a nurturer, gift-giver (in particular the gift of child-bearing fertility) and the preserver of family harmony. But this is superficial. To reach the depths of who and what she is, we must allow her image to come to life. She is not just mother, mermaid or ocean, womb or tomb; she is multidimensional. According to Hillman, the human psyche is also a whole that contains multiplicities.

Archetypal images have a life of their own and can be addressed on their own terms.

The emotional and visceral energy behind archetypal images is what makes them so potent when we in tap into them with our branding. When archetypes are encountered the numinous is experienced.

We each carry personal stories within us, alongside the collective stories that have been passed down through the ages. As you read through the chapters of this book, you will dip into the stories from the past and reflect on how you live and breathe these stories through your present experiences.

I'd like to tell you a true story from my personal past that reflects through into my own business and brand:

*I sank down to the bottom effortlessly. Floating down.*

*The crystal clear water and the silence felt calming. No confusion or chaos.*

As I sat at the bottom of the deep end of our pool in Encino, California, I wasn't afraid.

My dog Spokane stuck his snout into the pool, but he didn't jump in. I saw him running around the perimeter and could hear his barking, which sounded miles away.

It seemed like I sat there for an eternity.

"No one knows I'm in the pool. And I can't swim," I thought to myself. I searched myself for any twinge of fear or panic but nothing was there.

Last night there was a all-nighter that kept me up into the wee hours.

Another rock n' roll party has taken over my house at 2 o'clock in the afternoon. I came out here to get some peace and quiet. Why am I the old fuddy duddy at age four? It doesn't seem fair. I hate these parties; they keep me up all night.

Under the water there's a crystalline silence. The beating of my heart has slowed down to almost zero. I don't need to breathe or even think. Stay down here forever in my own quiet, glistening world.

But, there is a problem. I do need to rise eventually to get air.

Spokane was sticking his nose in the water. He was pointing to the steps. There was a metal ladder that I could jump up, grab onto and pull myself out.

What a great dog. He saved my life.

I jumped numerous times to reach the bottom rung of the ladder. Now, I speculate that there may have been invisible helping hands pushing me upwards to the air I needed to stay alive.

I emerged from the bottom and went to my room to dry off.

No one ever knew that it happened.

This story may sound tragic or sad to you. But it laid out the map for the rest of my life, and what I later turned into a branding triumph: embodying the mermaid archetype visually and textually.

My current love of mermaids, being near or in the water and the ability to sink deeply into silence is reflected in that childhood experience. As you do your own inner work as outlined in this book, you will find the clarity to begin to develop your own unique and enchanted brand.

## Archetypal Branding

In this book we will explore seven archetypal approaches to branding your business. We'll bring in the elements of magic, mysticism, mythology and marketing and branding ingenuity—through stories, memories, embodied experience and the seven chakras.

Each chapter provides a lens that will illuminate different aspects of yourself. You can read the chapters in the order that I present them or you can meander through, allowing your passions, interests and intuition to lead the journey. Each chapter stands on it's own, yet there is a reason for the particular chapter organization I devised.

While reading *Myths of Light: Eastern Metaphors of the Eternal* from the *Collected Works of Joseph Campbell*, I came upon a section of the book where he describes each of the seven major chakras and which archetypes and stories they connect to. I'd never put myth and the chakras together before; I became entranced with his ideas.

I'm emphasizing the manifesting path (heaven to earth) rather than the liberating path (earth to heaven) through my own personal preference and experience, so the first chapter of this book begins with the crown chakra at the top of the head, the seventh chakra called *Sahasrara* (thousand-petaled lotus) in Sanskrit.

Here there is complete bliss and no separation between the soul and source of all. I associate the theme of Sovereignty with this chakra and will bring in archetypes that support the functions of self-rulership in **Chapter 1: Rules of Enchantment**.

**Chapter 2: Memoir Mirror** is based on the sixth chakra, known as *Ajna* (command) and located at the brow. Here we encounter the archetypes that support wisdom and vision.

*Visuddha* (purifying one) located at the throat is the fifth major chakra and is associated with communication, messages and music, art and dance. **Chapter 3: Midrash Movement** focuses on how to communicate your truth and grants you that permission slip to rewrite your story, your way.

**Chapter 4: The Waters of Aphrodite** will flow you through the fourth chakra, *Anahata* (unstruck), the central chakra at the heart of the body. This is the place where the Divine reaches down to devotee and the devotee reaches upward. In Esoteric Sacred Magic, the heart center is where we directly access our magical imagination via the astral realm.

The astral realm is multi-vibrational and contains the thought forms and images before they are manifested on the physical plane. Here we can use the imagination to mold these thoughts and images into what we truly desire to manifest in the outer world. Our inner world is rich with treasures of the heart, mind and body. If we wish to mold the outer world to match the inner world, the astral realm is the spiritual plane that allows us to do this.

Later in this introductory chapter, I'll walk you through my methods of working with the figures and images in the astral realm.

Our next stop on the manifesting path is **Chapter 5: Shining Your Light** featuring the third chakra, called *Manipura* (city of the shining jewel) located at the solar plexus. Whatever you digest mentally, emotionally and physically contributes to the health of your ego; if your third chakra is in a weakened state you will suffer from sluggish energy and low self-esteem. If it's overactive you'll want to control everything at any cost.

When the energy is balanced and strong in the third chakra, we are warriors of light. We value ourselves and our contributions without trying to conquer others.

In **Chapter 6: Engaging the Trickster**, the second, pelvic or sacral, chakra named *Svadisthana* (sweetness) rules change, movement and sexuality. It may come as a surprise to some that I don't associate Aphrodite with *just* the second chakra. She is also the epitome of self-love and self-pleasure so I've placed her at the fourth chakra, the heart.

This chapter centers around Trickster, who doesn't want to be in complete control of her bodily urges. Here the impulse is to CREATE and INNOVATE. If we just stick to routines and only do what people expect from us, we eventually grow bored and our marketing reflects this. It's good to shake things up now and then... although some of the entrepreneurs I profile in this chapter have made it the norm to be unusual and even shocking in their brands.

We finally land at the first chakra in **Chapter 7: The Spiral Journey Home**, where we end and begin with the foundation of our identity and the seed of our gifts. This is the domain of *Muladhara* (root base), which houses the *kundalini*, the coiled, sleeping serpent also known as *Shakti*.

In this chapter we'll explore the world of Paulo Coelho's character Santiago in *The Alchemist* as a way of mapping your own journey as an entrepreneur using fresh eyes.

Once you complete the full introduction you can choose to begin at any of the chakras, even go through the chapters in reverse if that's what feels right to you.

The first seven chapters describing the chakras and their associated archetypes comprise the first section of the book, **A Mythological Journey Through the Seven Chakras**. The next section, **The Dark Side of Entrepreneurship**, features shadow work and the three taboo topics money, sex and power.

The **Resources and Recommended Reading** section will help you find more practical + inspirational support for you and your business. Don't skip it!

# Soul Work Is Alchemical

## Gathering your *prima materia*

*"If you went in search of it, you would not find the boundaries of the soul, though you traveled every road-so deep is its measure [logos]."*

**–Heraclitus**

To dive into the depths, is to enter the realm of the soul.

When we talk about work, career and livelihood, we are talking about Soul in action in the world.

Hillman, like Jung before him, postulates that if "psyche is image […] then why not go on to say, 'images are souls,' and our job with them is to meet them on that soul level" ("Inquiry" 81).

To brand with psyche at the forefront, is to bring into visibility your very Soul. Big stuff.

We often wait for someone or something to give us permission to follow *our* own true path. It's easier to follow someone else's example than to find out what lies within our hearts and follow that truth. This often stems from situations where we were made to feel ashamed of who we are or embarrassed about our beliefs.

Many of us were told as children to be seen and not heard, our voices completely choked off.

From adolescence through early adulthood, society pushes us out into the world with no rituals of self-hood or fortification. We long to be accepted, acknowledged, to love and be loved. We become human pretzels bending to match the desires of those around us. We lose our way, our path, our light and our voice.

It's no surprise that we follow the rules, disappear into the woodwork and are afraid to outshine others. It's my intention that the work you do in this book will help you formulate your own rules and allow your light to radiate your unique personality.

In each chapter I will demonstrate ways to begin working with your own materials by showing you how other entrepreneurs work with theirs. You are welcome to play with the same stories if they resonate with you—you can also reinterpret and revise them with your own palette of experiences. But I imagine, you'll find the most power in working with your own *prima materia*.

I visualize my roles throughout this book as:

> *Cosmic Cheerleader;*
>
> *Synthesizing Oracle;*
>
> *Mer Mistress of Play;*
>
> *and Center Holder.*

Even though I'm not sitting next to you as you read this, my intention is that *Return to Enchantment* will feel like a companion and guide along this stretch of your journey as an entrepreneur.

This process will take you into the **depths** of your soul.

As pleasurable as it can be, you will need **time** to go deep and then to integrate your insights through taking action and implementing what you learn. I know you're a powerhouse entrepreneur with an extremely busy schedule, possibly a family to care for and your own programs to run. For this immersive experience, you can set aside as much, or as little, time as you need to put towards it.

I promise you the rewards will outweigh the time you spend reading the book and engaging in its meditations, writing prompts and branding explorations.

Here are my tips and *suggestions* for how to best sail through each chapter:

1. Have a *Return to Enchantment* date day or night each week, when you can set aside 2-3 hours to dip into your stories, reflect on their significance and find ways to create

the material for your Mythic Brand (more on the MB in Chapter 1). Think of it as "Romancing your brand."

2. Keep a morning ritual as consistently as possible over the next few months. One of my methods for staying connected to my inner world is through Imaginative Play (known throughout the other modules as IP). I spend about 20-30 minutes in IP each morning downloading ideas and information. Often full blog posts will just pour through me afterwards. You may already have a similar practice in place, in which case keep doing what works for you.

3. Decide how long you will take for each chapter ahead of time. Try setting a goal of 10-14 days for each one, to allow yourself ample exploration time. However, if you think to yourself, "I'm getting soooo much out of working with the Trickster archetype (Chapter 6) right now that I have to stay with this!" Then stay with it! I'm here to advocate YOUR best process.

4. Keep in mind that the world, the brand, you're (re)creating is *play*. In other words, allow the new Mythic Brand time to morph, transform and take root before going out and getting a new logo, website design, new business name, etc. Often in our excitement at novel ideas we jump into the, "This is it!" mindset. While a-ha moments are essential to fuel your work, it's best to allow ample time to feel into the stability of your new brand before handing over your life savings to that website designer/developer. This New World may become the brand behind your external brand—the invisible source that is weaving into your life and business—that begins to radiate through your current brand. Your process and how you'll decide to work with your Mythic Brand will be unique from anyone else's.

5. Do this work with a partner for accountability and support. It's so much easier to do this work with a living, breathing witness who can mirror your desire for growth.

Should I share my experiences with others?

This is a hard one to answer. Some of the most well-meaning people say the most awful things from time to time—things that hurt our confidence or fill us with self-doubt. You'll be diving into NEW and vulnerable territory as you read this book. I think it's fine to share your process, ideas and insights with others as long as they are 100% supportive of your dreams, vision and goals.

What if there's no wayyy in hell I can spend 2-3 hours every week on branding and marketing play?

My theory is that the playing will help you flow with your creative and day-to-day work and be **more productive**. Even if you can only do 15 minutes per day, try it out and see.

How do I fit *everything* in and still maintain a sense of play?

Play first. Why is that? From the research that I've done, rewards systems do not work well. *"I'll play after I get my work done."*

We all know that almost never happens.

Think of play as another approach to work. You come at problems in a new way. Notice the patterns: circular, reverse, zig zag, sideways. Turn things upside down. Do the opposite of what you'd normally do.

What's the difference between play and vacation mind?

For our purposes they are not mutually exclusive and yet they are distinct.

*Vacation mind* = vacate, release, emptying.

*Play* = presence, engaging oneself, tending to.

Play first. Work later. Innovate more.

Your Mythic Brand will come to you in stages as you read this book. It is not a linear process; think of the journey as twisting, winding and serpentine.

You'll play within the themes of the seven different chapters and have a framework to mix and match your stories to various brand attributes that I will introduce.

There will be times when you feel elated that the exercises are clicking, followed by stretches of time when everything is murky and makes absolutely no fucking sense! This is the alchemical process in action. And it is absolutely perfect!

You'll find yourself (and your Mythic Brand) in the myth of Inanna, the tale of Psyche and Eros, in Tolkein's *Lord of the Rings* and JK Rowling's *Harry Potter* series… even *The Little Mermaid*.

Like Santiago winding his way through the world in *The Alchemist*, we will be on a journey to find our own deepest treasure.

**You** are that pot of gold, known in the Celtic world as the cauldron of Annwn.

Click your heels because like Dorothy from the *Wizard of Oz*, you're about to take the ultimate journey that leads *home*, to the center of your heart.

# My Definition of Brand

Of course, I want to begin by telling a story.

*How I became a mermaid.*

In 2011, I called my photographer and dear friend Rachel Sarah Thurston, of r.s.thurston photography, to ask her to photograph me as a mermaid. She just laughed. She had been obsessed with mermaids for two weeks before I even called her. We knew we were meant to work on this project together. Gave us both the goosebumps. I was so excited to begin and Rachel matched my energy and desire to manifest the vision.

More than just being photographed, I wanted to BE a mermaid. And I knew it would take more than a tail (don't have one since I'm not a fish) and long, glorious locks (which I do have).

I ordered a purple, sparkly mermaid's tail from eBay and about four months later, in February 2012, Rachel photographed me in the Watsu pool I trained in as well as on Hendry's beach in Santa Barbara.

So, what does this have to do with BRANDING?

In my mind… everything.

Branding is creating an image, then breathing life into it through expert implementation (in words, photos/images, design and color), with help from an amazing photographer like Rachel, for example. We shared a vision of what was possible with the Mermaid.

But the side of branding I want to talk about is its healing potential. I believed for many years, especially after working for *the man* for so long, that branding was about choosing the right color, words, images, attitude and emotions. But branding is psychological too. These are all obvious, on-the-surface reasons for why branding is important.

Not until after the mermaid shoot did I realize that I was not only breathing into my future mermaid-inspired memoir or great photos for my website… something deeper was trying to emerge, to become embodied.

I showed up for my shoot with unmanicured toenails and fingernails; I hadn't even shaved my legs! (I was, after all, going to hide them inside my phony tail.) My stomach was bloated from premenstrual water retention and a night of gorging on Rusty's Pizza.

It still blows my mind that I would eat half a pizza the night before a photo shoot. What was I thinking?!

In fact, my lack of adornment or desire to look and feel my best was a reflection of my vulnerability around self-image and my lack of self-love; the two feelings that hit me when I feel exposed and uncomfortable. Rachel, however, assured me I looked gorgeous, bless her heart. One of my other dearest friends Lisa Beck was also on hand to help me hop around the sand in my tail! During the shoot she smiled and encouraged me. I was so blessed to have Lisa there. If only we could "beam in" our best friends every time we feel insecure!

After seeing the photos and watching the slideshow Rachel created I had tears in my eyes. This was me! But, not me. We had co-created an archetypal representation of the energy that had been in my life, living under the surface since I was a child.

Becoming the mermaid I encountered in my visionary work, was healing for me. It empowered me. And, branding myself as a mermaid has made me begin to look *archetypally* at myself and at this image that has haunted my consciousness.

# Methods of Inner Work

## About Imaginative Play

Imaginative Play (IP) is adapted from Jung's process of dialoguing with our unconscious selves, called Active Imagination (AI). AI is primarily a psychological practice that involves intense engagement with the figures of your inner life. One of the differences between Imaginative Play and Active Imagination is that in IP we consciously choose which being we want to work with. In AI you allow the voices to come spontaneously, without setting any intention of who you are speaking to. AI also requires that you meet with a particular being (or set of them) each day at the same time, for months or years. IP is the perfect way to get your feet wet in this practice and get nearly the same benefits.

IP allows parts of you that have been denied, repressed or forgotten to have a voice. The practice involves relaxing deeply and emptying your mind, except for a specific intention. The voices of your unconscious bubble up to be heard and seen by your conscious mind.

The imagination is the sacred space where the Divine inhabits us.

The archetypal power of a goddess or god would short circuit our nervous systems if we had direct contact with them. For example when Zeus revealed himself in al his glory to Semele, mortal mother of Dionysus, she exploded from his intense brilliance.

Archetypal images (in the form of deities and inner world beings) reach us in the middle ground, in the realm of imagination, or *mundus imaginalis*, a term coined by the French philosopher and Islamicist Henry Corbin. This intermediate world is located between the empirical and intellectual, abstract realms.

> [...] the world of the image, the *mundus imaginalis*: a world that is ontologically as real as the world of the senses and

that of the intellect. This world requires its own faculty of perception, namely, imaginative power, a faculty with a cognitive function, a *noetic* value which is as real as that of sense perception or intellectual intuition. We must be careful not to confuse it with the imagination identified by so-called modern man with "fantasy," and which, according to him, is nothing but an outpour of "imaginings." (Corbin 5)

IP builds a bridge to *mundus imaginalis* that allows us to meet these archetypal forces with ease and safety.

## Benefits of Imaginative Play

- Reduces overwhelm, exhaustion, burnout

- Reduces feelings of being disconnected or alienated

- Increases confidence in your decisions

- Increases creativity, you play a more active role than in traditional meditation

- Transforms your business, alchemical integration

**My personal morning ritual involves connecting and dialoguing with my inner figures for 20 minutes. I find my day runs a lot smoother if I do this. I'd love for you to try IP at least 5 times after reading this chapter.**

You choose who you would like to work with during this time. You can work with your Muse, Angels, Guides, Mermaids. I'll also mention that in this early stage of our process, it's super beneficial to begin connecting with your Inner Mentor or Guru (*guru* means "one who dispels the darkness"). Try connecting with this source at least once or twice during this first two weeks. Make contact so that when you need the advice and guidance of your Inner Guru it will flow to you easily.

## Exploration: Connect with your Inner Guru through Imaginative Play

1. Close your eyes and begin to slow down your breath. Take deep and gentle breaths all the way into your belly. Send your consciousness deep into the core of your body. I often set it inside the bowl of my pelvis, visualized as a transmutational cauldron or a chalice of sparkling water.

2. Ask your Inner Guru to come forward for your initial dive into IP.

3. Greet your inner world being and ask what they'd like to share with you in this moment. Like any good conversation, don't start by interrogating your inner friend with dozens of questions. They'll close down just like a person would. Be a good listener, just like a good friend would be.

4. When it feels right, begin to ask questions or for advice that you need in your projects, business and life. You can ask for more clarification if it is needed and you may also disagree or question the advice if something doesn't feel right to you. You have the right to your own point of view. Your inner world being will find an appropriate solution in cooperation with you. This is a collaboration, not a one-way conversation.

5. Write down the entire interaction in your journal or on your computer as it is happening. Often I'll write the inner world being's initial/s then a ":" and what they said, followed by my initial and my response. It looks a bit like a script with who said what intermixed with my feelings and sensations during the encounter.

# Embodiment Practices + Explorations

Each chapter will have prompts, meditations, chakra breathing exercises and a body prayer at the end. These will help you deepen into the archetypal theme of the chapter and put its concepts into practice.

## How to Practice Imaginative Play

Begin by slowing down your breath. If you use a regimen to center your mind and relax your body, do this now. I recommend learning the **Fourfold Breath** combined with **Chakra Breathing** for this purpose.

## How to Do the Fourfold Breath

Settle into your inner space of silence. Breath in deeply and slowly for four counts, hold for four, breathe out slowly and gently for four counts and hold for another four counts. Keep repeating this pattern for about 2 minutes (or longer if it feels right). The Fourfold Breath has a spirallic effect on your body, mind and soul. You'll find yourself relaxed and as centered as a deeply-rooted tree.

## How to Do Chakra Breathing

I incorporated chakra work into the first seven chapters of this branding book because it is one of the easiest and fastest ways to transform your inner and outer worlds.

I begin with the seventh chakra in Chapter 1 and work my way down to the root chakra in Chapter 7. This brings heaven to earth, to focus on the manifesting path of the Divine Will as it works through your brand.

Each chapter will outline the instructions for breathing into each chakra. I like to feel the breath coming in to nourish and purify each chakra. When holding the breath, see the chakra growing in size and radiance. On the exhale, breathe its colorful energy into your aura to cleanse and replenish your etheric field.

Endeavor to do the chakra work as often as you can throughout the course of reading this book. In the morning is ideal and whenever you need a relaxed energy boost.

## Active Reading

Reading is transformative, especially when we consciously interact with the material. If you're just reading passively for diversion and entertainment, you might learn a few things but you won't be transformed.

Read to experience transformation! It rocks.

Practice each meditation, chakra breathing and body prayer at least once and see how it feels. If it feels right, practice more.

Bring your imagination into it. If you're trying on your Sovereignty shoes for the first time, do the Triumph body prayer in Chapter 1 as if you are a Queen or King. Being present to the archetype will feel potent and palpable.

Be what it is that you imagine in your heart.

It's time to embark on a new journey to the center of your heart and imagination.

And as with all journeys, we begin by crossing the threshold, turning the page.

**Once upon a time...**

# Chapter 1: The Rules of Enchantment

*"There's nothing you can do that's more important than being fulfilled. You become a sign, you become a signal, transparent to transcendence; in this way you will find, live, and become a realization of your own personal myth."*

**–Joseph Campbell**

When it comes to being fulfilled as an entrepreneur we need to begin at SOVEREIGNTY.

Before we dive into the qualities of the Sovereign, I want to clarify its function: this archetype is the vision holder and boundary setter for its Queendom or Kingdom. The king or queen makes the final decisions in all matters that are related to the vision and safety of the realm.

Let's be clear: the Sovereign is not a manager. Sovereigns do not manage people or enforce boundaries. That is a manager's job.

There are many managers but only ONE sovereign.

As the Sovereign of your realm, keep this in mind. When you begin to micromanage and do everything in your business out of guilt or habit, STOP. Focus on the growth and nourishment of your vision. If you neglect this aspect of your business, get ready for burnout. Your business' growth will be stunted too. Your actions will not be inspired by the vision your business holds; you'll just be going through the motions of acting like an entrepreneur. (Or what you've been told an entrepreneur "should" be doing.)

Being an entrepreneur is another ballgame altogether.

Many of us are confronted with is the need to wear many hats in our businesses. Without the income to hire a project manager or virtual assistant we have to take on the roles and tasks of many people. I deal with this by creating a regularly scheduled day for visioning the future of my business and reflecting on important decisions. Monday is ruled by the moon and is perfect for visioning and reflecting, I set aside that day to do this aspect of my work. I am Sovereign on Mondays. I take no clients on this day. It's mine.

Choose a day and time to act as the Sovereign of your realm. Protect this space and be in it consistently. This will help you feel connected to the Soul of your business and help prevent overwhelm.

### "Should I follow the rules or follow my heart?"

This is a question I've asked myself many times throughout my life.

Give yourself permission to be sovereign over your own life and business. I know this sounds totally cray-cray, but we often wait for someone to give us permission… to set our own rates, working hours and decide how often to send our newsletter.

I certainly don't think of myself as a rule breaker kind of a gal. I like to follow trusted and tried wisdom. The mystic priestess within allows me to enjoy conversing with spiritual guides to help me through this labyrinth of entrepreneurship. My guides are mostly elemental in nature—fae and mer in particular—but I've had breakthroughs come from my Angels, Nemetona, Yemaya and Morgen. (Nemetona is the Goddess of Sacred Groves, Yemaya is the Mother of Unconditional Love and is the ocean itself. Morgen is the Sovereign Lady of Avalon.)

I create my own rituals, rules and regulations in accordance with my body's and the Earth's energies. I would love for you to do the same. Being an entrepreneur shouldn't mean having to work yourself into ill health and exhaustion.

After leaving my corporate life in 2011, I found that I became frustrated with the self-employment systems I put in place. I felt like a prisoner in my self-made cell of continuous blogging, networking, marketing and emailing. I was physically, emotionally and spiritually spent.

And I wasn't seeing immediate results that I expected from all of my hard work.

But there was a hell of a lot going on under the surface.

At some point, without realizing it, my numbers doubled on Twitter and Facebook and my newsletter list tripled.

The moolah was increasing too. My gross revenue increased 400% from 2012 to 2013!

Every offering needed many, many hours of marketing work: running campaigns, drafting the "perfect" sales page, planning and writing three or more corresponding blog posts and at least one dedicated email, two or three videos, four or more short Tweetables…

**The list goes on and on.**

**Exhausting.**

And when our results (sales, likes, tweets, signups) don't match our expectations, we tend to throw it all back on ourselves:

> *"What did I do wrong?"*
>
> *"I didn't start promoting soon enough."*
>
> *"I can't do this right."*
>
> *"I'm terrible at marketing/promoting."*
>
> *"No one has money/can afford to pay."*
>
> *"No one wants what I have to offer."*
>
> *"My sales page was off."*
>
> *"I looked like a jackass in my videos."*

All of these stories in our minds are exactly that, ***stories***. It's time to stop beating ourselves up over things we have absolutely 0% control over, such as how many people sign up for our eCourses.

There's one thing we have 100% control over: **we can always tell a new story.**

**Your brand contains a story: a narrative that has multiple themes and usually more than one core message. It can be complex or it can be simple.**

Your brand and your marketing reflect the stories you love and consciously or unconsciously live by. Becoming more conscious of the archetypal energy behind everything you experience not only brings more meaning to what you do, but also helps others CONNECT to that meaning. They will hire you and buy your products and services based on feeling a resonance with *you* (which is to say, your brand.)

Yes, it's time to **kneel at the altar of You**. More specifically, a sovereign, sassy and playful you.

We are given plenty of opportunities to consider how to "improve" ourselves, our marketing and our sales. But there is no such thing as perfecting the Soul.

You emerged from your mother's womb whole and spectacular, filled with limitless possibilities. **You are perfection.**

You are as vast as the widest and deepest sea. Just the thought of our big-ness makes us all the more humble.

The fact that there is only one of you in all of space and time makes your brand rare and exquisite.

Take a deep breath right now and celebrate *that*!

When you pray and/or meditate as you're working through this chapter, kneel. Place your forehead on the ground. Feel your spaces open wide to celebration.

Every time you celebrate and honor your being, you empty out the old and allow in the new. Cultivate deep humility at the altar of your Soul. Let the Sovereign of you, in whatever form, show itself.

# Your Mythic Brand

Let's define **brand**.

First and foremost, branding reflects personal clarity. Knowing your role in the world and how you and your company function in this role is the backbone of your brand. Your *why* is the heartbeat. The colors, fonts and iconography are the skin.

Your brand is represented by your behavior: how you promote yourself. How you interact on social media and in Facebook groups leaves an indelible impression. Messaging and projects that are consistent with your brand build trust. (And help to increase your newsletter list and bank account. In my world, money is sacred too.)

Behavior, messaging, your why, your style—all of these create an emotional bond with your audience. It's *that* bond that compels them to open your emails and purchase what you have to offer.

Your dream clients and customers do not make purchases just based on rational decisions. They buy from you because endorphins are released when they read your sales page and are tantalized by its story.

You want to leave a legacy. Tell a story that moves, inspires and heals.

Go beyond making the world a better place. Create a new one.

*That*, my friend, is a Mythic Brand.

## What is your Mythic Brand model?

Some examples:

- **God/dess-Like Celebrity** (examples: Danielle LaPorte, Marie Forleo, Oprah, Angelina Jolie) :: Personal mojo, expert status, author/ity: who you are stands at the forefront of your brand.

- **Behind-the-Scenes Biz Mogul** (examples: Virgin, Apple, Microsoft, E!) :: Your business stands on its own and is not specifically focused on your personality. Can operate without you, yet reflects your personal values.

- **Weaving-the-Web Systems Wizard** (examples: Total Product Blueprint, Conscious Introvert Success, Paid to Exist) :: Your core message and offering is made into its own proprietary system or suite of products and services.

Each of these categories has areas of overlap. The idea is to start building your realm with a solid foundation based on the brand archetype you long to express.

Set your timer for **15 minutes** for this section:

- Create a name and description for the kind of brand you are developing… and focus more on what is stirring inside you rather than what you think your brand should be or do.

- It can be wildly creative or exuberantly quiet. This is a direct expression of your Soul.

- What is longing to be expressed through you and your business?

Congratulations! You're done with this initial deep dive.

Myth Magic Wizardry   Mytic Mystery
w) Systems / Blueprints        Poetry
Not a goodie two-shoes
Dark/mysterious edge
Seer/fortune teller  Gypsy
energy

# The Queen Archetype: Inanna

*"If you're the Queen, why are you acting like the scullery maid?"*

This is what Inanna asked me when I was engaged in an imaginative dialogue with her one afternoon.

Eight thousand years ago in ancient Mesopotamia, the myth of Inanna was widely known and 3,000-4,000 years ago the myth was written down in cuneiform on tablets by female priestesses.

A quickie lesson on the myth of Inanna's descent.

Inanna, whose name means "The Lady of Heaven," hears a call from the Underworld, which is ruled by her sister Queen Ereshkigal. To get to her sister in the deepest bowels of the earth, Inanna must pass through seven gates. At each gate she gives up a piece of the queenly raiment that symbolizes her status as royalty and a woman of society.

> *From the "great above" she set her mind toward the "great below,"*
>
> *The goddess, from the "great above" she set her mind toward the "great below,"*
>
> *Inanna, from the "great above" she set her mind toward the "great below."*
>
> *My lady abandoned heaven, abandoned earth,*
>
> *To the nether world she descended...*

Her crown is the first object she gives up.

When she reaches the underworld, she is completely naked and stripped of her all titles. Her sister, on the floor writhing in pain, "fixes" her eye upon Inanna, which kills her. Inanna's lifeless body is placed on a meat hook to rot.

Ereshkigal's husband has just died; she is in mourning and possibly in labor with a child. Some scholars say that she is actually getting ready to rebirth Inanna.

Ninshibur, Inanna's faithful lady-in-waiting, knows something has gone wrong; Inanna had told Ninsibur to get help for her if she failed to return within three days. To gather help, Ninshibur runs to the various Sky Gods, but they refuse to rescue Inanna, for her *hubris* was too great in their judgmental eyes. Only the god of wisdom and water, Enki, shows compassion for the plight of Inanna, sending his emissaries to the underworld to rescue her.

The two creatures sent by Enki as emissaries reach out to Ereshkigal by showing her compassion. Each time Ereshkigal moans out in pain, the creatures echo her. This makes her feel acknowledged. Her heart softens and she releases the body of Inanna.

Inanna is restored by Enki's creatures who give her the food and water of life. She returns to the upper world to take her place as queen again.

Your *Return to Enchantment* journey begins at the very source of self-rulership: your divinely bestowed Sovereignty works from the top down. As you open your crown chakra and your life to bringing in Divine Source, you align with the Cosmos, the earth and your Soul star. The Soul star—your undying essence—is the queen or king.

As we embark on a descent into the body itself, infusing every cell with the radiance of the life force, we ally with our Shadow living in the Underworld. We embrace and kiss that aspect of self that is suffering in physical or emotional pain, raging with anger and resentful for being unacknowledged and forgotten. The kiss, the silvery light of the Cosmos, enters the crown chakra and flows it's way down, down, down. The light glows in our darkest spaces, warming the ice and allowing its gentle glow to permeate them.

Like Inanna's descent into the Underworld to meet her dark, Shadow sister Ereshkigal, you'll meet your own innermost core self, the shadow sibling that you may have been neglecting for years.

Our sovereignty is ancient. The archetypal queen is an archaic part of ourselves that we access through the body and through visioning. The crown chakra (the 7th major chakra located at the top of the head) is the living energetic symbol of our birthright to rule over ourselves. But, from the time we are born we are conditioned to doubt our inner authority and take on the laws of external forces that do not serve our growth or fulfillment.

As we grow older and wiser we begin to identify and cast off the shackles of outworn rules, dead stories and sabotaging behaviors—re-learning how to listen to our intuition and the wisdom of our bodies.

# Myth of Sovereignty: The Loathsome Lady

This retelling is a story from Arthurian legends about the marriage of Sir Gawain to Lady Ragnell.

Arthur is hunting in the forest when a man, Sir Gromer, steps out of the shadows and threatens to have Arthur's head unless he can come back in one year and one day with the correct answer to one question:

"Tell me what it is that women desire most, above all else."

On his travels Arthur searches for the answer, and with only one month left, King Arthur meets a woman covered in jewels and gold. She is disfigured and ugly.

She reveals her name, Lady Ragnell, and tells him that she is the only one who can help him find the answer to the riddle. However in return for this information Arthur must agree to give her something she wants.

He agrees.

"Grant me the knight Sir Gawain to wed. Either I marry him, or you must lose your head."

She continues, "…now I will divulge what women desire above all else. Some men say we desire to be beautiful, or that we desire men's attention, or that we desire to be well wed. These men do not know the truth. What we desire above everything else is to have sovereignty, to rule our lives as we see fit, and not be beholden to another. Go forth, King Arthur, for your life is spared."

Arthur returns to Camelot with the bride-to-be. Sir Gawain must take one for the team.

Of course Gawain, a noble knight, doesn't even hesitate. He vows to marry the hideous creature without flinching.

Arthur wants them to marry at a time when no one will show up to see Lady Ragnell's ugliness. She refuses. They must be wed in the open for ALL to see.

In the post-wedding boudoir, she asks Gawain to kiss her and when he turns around he sees a beautiful young woman standing before him!

She tells him that she was under a curse placed by Sir Gromer, her brother: she is ugly by day and her beautiful self at night.

As her husband Gawain will have to choose: does he want her beautiful by day and ugly at night, or monstrous by day and glorious at night?

He turns to her and says, "To have you beautiful at night and no more, would grieve my heart. And if I desire to have you fair during the day, then I'm sure I could not bear the night. I put the choice in your own hands. Whatever you choose, to be beautiful by day or by night, as your husband that choice will be my own."

Poof! The curse is broken.

Lady Ragnell remains beautiful day and night... and they live happily ever after.

Because Sir Gawain was willing to allow his wife her sovereignty, BEAUTY was restored.

# Case Study, Danielle LaPorte

*"A mythical bird that never dies, the phoenix flies far ahead to the front, always scanning the landscape and distant space. It represents our capacity for vision, for collecting sensory information about our environment and the events unfolding within it. The phoenix, with its great beauty, creates intense excitement and deathless inspiration."*

**–Master Lam Kam Chuen,** *The Feng Shui Handbook*

Like the Phoenix who rises from the ashes of its own death, Danielle rose from the corpse of her own company, severed her biz partnership (and I believe her love partnership as well) and recreated herself from zero.

After working one-on-one with hundreds of clients, she released *The Fire Starter Sessions* in 2010 to rave reviews and thousands of sales. The stuff of entrepreneurial legend.

Danielle is the quintessential Phoenix. She burned her old branding (White Hot Truth) and went straight into her white-hot essence: DanielleLaPorte.com.

All of a sudden everyone wanted to brand their own name. Yes, including me.

Over the past four years, she has redesigned her website at least three times by my count.

Her redesign, which launched December 4, 2013 (one day before her self-published version of *The Desire Map* was released), was the most stripped down she version to date. Lots of white space. The way she likes it.

Ms. LaPorte's writing has a definitive mystic flavor, and is deeply poetic. Mystics have come from every religious tradition—Rumi from the Sufi, Azriel of Gerona from Kaballah, Hildegard von Bingen from Christianity, to cite just a few examples.

We are looking at a High Priestess of entrepreneurship. Who else can tell us to create Stop Doing lists, or to sit in a hot tub instead of in front of the computer, and get away with it?

The High Priestess manifests by being, not doing and especially not by overdoing. She's able to go after what she desires by feeling through her heart, not by over-analyzing in her head.

Danielle released *The Desire Map* after a month long pre-launch of onboarding affiliates and releasing riveting teaser videos. Her look in the videos was much softer than ever. It reminded me of the soft-focus filter of moonbeams.

Seated on a leather couch, she beckons us to enter a world where we can accept our desires and live by their power and purity. Think Rita Hayworth with a touch of Bjork. Pure, stripped down glamour alongside avant garde artistry.

What Danielle models so beautifully is how to bridge the gap between you and your livelihood, so they more than overlap. They become one and the same. Unity. The two flames become one.

I see Danielle LaPorte as not only a model of the successful female entrepreneur, but as a sacred teacher. Who knew that I could be my happy mystical self and still have affluence?

Danielle says:

> "Authenticity is risky business, for sure. I think you need to know the rules in order to break them, otherwise it just gets flaky. You can write in your own voice, but you need to be a decent writer. You can hammer out an unconventional business plan, but you better know the key components that go into a traditional plan...

> "I think that mere rebellion and anger are slippery slopes in terms of blogging. Personally, I'm not a fan of many diarists or activist bloggers. I feel I owe it to my audience to refine my crap, and think it through into something instructional and/ or inspiring.

**Authentic + responsible = useful. I like useful.**" (May 2010
interview with Jen Louden)

*(Danielle's case study first appeared on Rebelle Society.)*

# The Rules of Enchantment

- Act like the Sovereign of your realm, not the scullery maid. (You, and you alone, are responsible for every decision you make; you can build a council of any size to help you, i.e., a gang or a sidekick.)

- Make your own laws (work hours, types of projects undertaken, vacation length + frequency.)

- Name + define your realm. (Name its essence, define its topography and boundary lines.)

**When you create your Mythic Brand, use these guiding questions to steer you back to your soul:**

1. Who is your **Inanna**... what are you reaching for and what is your guiding star?

2. Who is your **Ereshkigal** or your version of the **Sky Gods**... a challenger or nemesis who brings out the best in you?

3. Who is your **Ninshibur**... supporters who will go to the ends of the earth to help you thrive?

4. What is your Mythic Brand's origin story?

Just about every story has the backstory, how it came to be. Think of Theogeny, Genesis, Rangi + Papa, Yggdrasil (World Tree), and Enuma Elish to name some of the hundreds, perhaps thousands, of creation myths.

**Create your own brief brand Cosmology in 5-10 sentences.**

- How was your brand born?

- What were the circumstances that brought it into being?

These make great stories for the "about" pages of your website.

The visioning and creating we do in *Return to Enchantment* is So. play. And as I'm sure you've heard before, success as an entrepreneu. is an inside job.

Sales and marketing do not have to feel sleazy, gross, or manipulative. You have something amazing to offer the world. You need to tell people about it. If you don't, you risk robbing someone of that magical genius that only you can share with them. We each have a unique gift and when we hold back, we hold others back. I know this sounds harsh, but it's true. Withholding your inner power, in the form of your gifts, puts you out of alignment and projects a weak template. When you model empowerment and are fully self-expressed, guess what? You give everyone else permission to do the same.

# Primacy of Play

The best way to re-center is to allow yourself more time for meandering in the inner imaginative and outer physical spaces, without attachment to any outcome.

It's so easy to fill ourselves with all kinds of stuff, thoughts and objects.

**Spaciousness leaves room for play. Do not rush to fill your spaces, internal + external.**

The term *reverie* originally meant "wild conduct, frolic," from Old French reverie "revelry, raving, delirium," from *resver* "to dream, wander, rave," of uncertain origin (also the root of rave). Meaning "daydream," is first attested in the 1650s.

Daydreaming is the backbone of **vacation mind** and the essential ingredient for producing any work of genius.

## Practice Daydreaming

For the next two weeks, schedule daydreaming time into your calendar. For some of your daydream sessions plan to be in an enclosed space, like your bedroom or a garden. For other daydream sessions visit public parks, coffee houses, art galleries, the beach or a forest. Wander about as if in a dream. (Just look both ways before crossing the street!)

Take along your journal because you will have plenty of ah-ha moments and prosperous ideas will flow effortlessly to you.

Vacation mind is how your brain functions when you are worry and stress free, relaxed, sipping on mojitos on the beach in Cancun. Vacation mind applied at work can profoundly improve productivity.

*"So what does it look like when you apply vacation mind to work? You let go of the anxiety. You aren't worried about getting it all done, or doing the right thing right now, or all the things you have to do later. You are immersed in enjoying whatever you've chosen to do right now."*

**−Leo Babauta, "The Practice of Work Mind & Vacation Mind, Simultaneously"**

## Stop Multitasking Mania

One morning per week choose only one priority task and spend the day completing it. Do not multi-task for a whole day. Almost every person I know who does this ends up finishing their one priority by lunchtime or before and then can decide to tackle any other tasks… or take the rest of the day off!

The other benefit to working this way is that you can complete the loop on a task or project and close the door. Clean energy. No leaks. Having too many unfinished projects at once depletes you. Worry and anxiety are two of the main culprits of entrepreneur burnout.

# Interview, Karen Tate

*You're a Goddess Advocate, Author, Radio Show Hostess and Tour Director… you focus on the Sacred Feminine and her place in contemporary and ancient herstory.*

*Even though you are a lover of the many faces of Goddess, I believe you have a special affinity for the Egyptian Goddess Isis. Can you tell us how Her sovereignty and Queendom have inspired your life and work?*

I grew up in a Catholic family in the Bible Belt of New Orleans, LA. My grandma had several garden and indoor altars to Mary, mother of Jesus and in Catholic school is was typical we would ceremoniously place wreaths on the head of Mary on her holy days. Couple that with my unique interest in foreign lands, particularly Egypt.

I can remember as a young girl, one of the most culturally fulfilling activities of my life was when a visiting exhibit of the King Tut exhibit came to New Orleans. I stood in line more than four hours with my brown bag lunch to see the exhibit. I suspect Isis was there on my shoulder for a long time, waiting for the perfect moment to awaken me to Her.

At first I was interested in Isis because she felt like such an accessible Goddess. During her life she was many things—lover, wife, widow, queen and single mother. She'd been betrayed by her husband and sister, so knew pain and grief. I felt she could understand one's hopes, fears and desires and answer our prayers. She was the loving mother so many of us might not have had in our own mortal mothers. In fact, Isis and her son, Horus, were the images Christianity co-opted when the church tried to sweep away Goddess from the world and replace her with with Mary and Jesus.

Later, when Isis as deity morphed into Isis as ideal or archetype,

I realized she personified so many qualities I held dear. She was a leader. Her symbol is the throne. It was she who gave the pharaoh the right to rule, using the laws of another Goddess, Maat, or truth and justice. We've heard the saying the power behind the throne—well, she was the throne with all the power and responsibility it entailed. She and her husband Osiris, archetypes of partnership, were said to create civilization and man and woman to love each other. This was so very different than patriarchal Christianity that marginalized women and conditioned females to be in service to men, ashamed of their sexuality and told that due to Eve's sin, all women deserved to suffer.

I guess you might say I saw Isis as a strong, caring, sharing, leader—an early feminist. She was independent. Sovereign. She was an example of woman standing on her own two feet and following her passion and vision. I saw her story as an example of how women's roles might have been different had patriarchy not been so successful sweeping the Great Mother and her many stories and myths from the world stage and therefore our psyches and cultures. The early years of my Goddess path were spent learning about Isis, visiting her sacred sites, and leading public rituals in her honor. I even dedicated my first book to her and the Egyptian God, Thoth.

I've felt Isis as deity, archetype and ideal, embrace me in her golden wings, for about thirty years now. I can't think of a better place to be.

### How does being a Sovereign Goddess woman show up in your professional life? How do you make critical decisions?

I think as we gain wisdom we learn it's a dance where sometimes you lead and other times you follow, depending on what the circumstances call for. We learn to trust our own judgment and vision or know when to ask for guidance. I think Isis, along with Sekhmet, the lion-headed Egyptian Goddess, have taught me tenacity, strength and determination.

I understand about going with the flow, listening and not trying to push a boulder uphill because that's a sure sign maybe I'm going down the wrong path. I've learned the challenges in life are really gifts that have steeled me, taught me, helped define me. I learned about the liberation of surrender and forgiveness. One of the most important things I believe has come from my Goddess knowledge is how our desire for perfection can be a detriment to getting anything done. We have to have the confidence to learn as we go and not be fearful we won't achieve perfection. I also have learned to like myself and be in my own skin and not look for the approval of others for my validation or self worth. As I've gotten older, moved into my Queen phase of life, I don't let people back me into corners and instead speak up, even if it's not politically correct.

*Isis is often invoked by women who feel like they're juggling too much, career, family, personal needs and spirituality. She is an archetypal figure AND she is ever present in a very tangible way.*

*Do you find that by honoring her place in your life and work that she empowers you to seek more balance, within and without?*

I'm a serious multi-tasker. I simultaneously work full time, take care of a husband and my two feline daughters, run my radio show of eight years, have written four books and give talks, teach classes and lead sacred journeys—one coming up next year is rto sacred sites of Turkey.

I think the many roles of a Goddess show a woman the many things she can be, sometimes simultaneously, sometimes at different phases of her life. That said, it is important not to overextend oneself. The ancient Egyptians were ever-fearful of imbalance which leads to chaos. So I guess from that perspective, we see how being out of balance can lead us to a lack of harmony and more stress which might lead to health issues and a depletion of our creativity and energy.

Goddess as Nature or Mother Earth also teaches us the importance of balance. If we have imbalance in eco-systems, we see loss of life and unhealthy conditions arising.

We, our lives and bodies are a microcosm of the macrocosm.

## What does Sovereignty mean to you as an Entrepreneur?

I guess it means being the Captain of my own ship. I don't have to defer to anyone, please anyone, meet some male boss' expectations, but it also means all the responsibility is on my shoulders so I'd better marshal all my talent, vision, energy and magic to get the job done and done well.

I don't have anyone but myself to blame for failure—or success!

I have the responsibility for how things are done, for the people I work with or who work with me. In a way it's like being a responsible Mother or Queen archetype. I think it also means as women we have to work harder to empower other women and not compete.

As we have a responsibility to change the world, we want to replace the status quo with a new normal that works for the most of us—particularly women who have been disadvantaged and undervalued for way too long. I think it's also about bringing new ways of doing things into the world and workplace—ideals of collaboration, partnership and negotiation.

# Practice: Media Cleanse + Sabbatical

Stay off of other people's blogs, no matter how good they are. Take time away from social media. Work from your bathtub, the beach, your backyard, your soft, comfy bed. Daydream a lot.

I know that we all need to promote our offerings and that many of us are leading Facebook groups and our own workshops/courses. Do the best that you can to stop any habits of over-consumption; media and others' ideas and rules are great for them, but ultimately can push you off your center.

Decide how often and how long you desire to stay off of social media, blogs and the computer.

Create a media cleanse and sabbatical that feels awesome to you and schedule it into your calendar today.

## Planning Your Social Media, Blog, Online Cleanse + Sabbatical

1.  How long will your media sabbatical/cleanse be? You can take half days, whole days, weeks or months. You decide.

2.  Choose the dates and mark them in your calendar.

3.  What and whom do you plan to avoid, ignore and release over that time? Make a list and your own set of rules to follow.

    Ideas: No social media, except to check in once daily to respond to friends, family, current clients and potential clients; check email no more than twice per day; turn off the cell phone for part of the day; turn on invisibility mode in Skype and let clients know they can contact you after lunchtime.

4. Prepare for your sabbatical by setting up marketing with Hootsuite. Inform anyone who may need to reach you during this period (family, friends and clients) that you'll get back to them at the time you've set aside for appointments. Put an autoresponder in place.

# Exploration: Connect with Your Favorite Stories

*"... stories are somehow alive, conscious and responsive to human emotions and wishes."*

**–Christopher Vogler,** *The Writer's Journey: Mythic Structure for Writers*

**Step 1: Immerse yourself.** Watch movies, read books (yes, even children's illustrated books you once loved), listen to your favorite songs. Pay attention to the parts that are meaningful for you. Take notes.

**Step 2: Study your notes.** Then answer these inquiries:

- What do you see of your own life reflected in the characters and plots?

- Did you connect with certain themes? How can these themes be expressed more in your life + work?

- What did the characters you loved in these stories desire in the beginning? How was their desire fulfilled?

**Step 3: Imagine.** Take a current or past business conundrum and write down the bare bones facts—who, what, where. Now, write a story about it using one of your favorite characters. How would they solve the problem? Be creative and make shit up! Have fun with it and throw away ideas of reality and practicality.

**Step 4: Reflect.** Can you apply a similar approach to problems that come up in the future?

# Meditation + Breathwork

**Focus**: Chakra 7, Crown Chakra

**Sanskrit**: Sahasrara, Thousandfold, thousand petaled lotus

**Associations**: Consciousness, Divinity, Sovereignty, Heaven, Cosmos, Violet Ray, Angelic Realm and Ascended Self.

**Planet**: Uranus

**Day of the Week**: Saturday

**Archetypes**: Inanna, Isis, Shiva, Zeus, Queen/King, Empress/Emperor, Archangels (particularly Michael)

For the next week or two, tend to the Starry Universal Realms and the intelligence of the Mythic Cosmos through your **7th chakra, located at the crown**.

Step 1: Begin by breathing white-violet colored light from the Cosmos into the center of the 1,000 petaled lotus at the top of your head.

Step 2: As you hold your breath for four counts after the inhale, see the light and energy from this chakra expanding and growing.

Step 3: When you exhale, breathe the violet-white light out of the petals and into your aura, which surrounds your entire body.

Step 4: Hold your breath for four counts visualizing the violet-colored light infusing your aura and bathing every cell of your body.

Repeat the pattern beginning with step 1 at least three more times.

For the final exhale, to end the practice, move the light and energy down your body and into the heart of Gaia (Earth Mother Goddess) with your breath. This will ground you for the Imaginative Play (IP) practice to follow.

## Spend time in Imaginative Play

For the duration of your work in this chapter dialogue with a favorite character that you identified during your explorations with your personal mythology.

What messages are they sending you?

How do you feel during and after the practice?

What synchronicities show up in the outer world that match the feeling or essence of the communication with your inner world beings?

## Body Prayer

This simple body prayer movement sequence will help you embody the energy of Sovereignty.

First close your eyes and imagine a radiant crown on the top of your head. Hold your spine even straighter, head even higher. Keep your face soft. Drop your shoulders. Relax all the muscles in your body. Being confident and strong does not mean you have to be tense.

You are holding the stance of the Queen or King, Empress or Emperor.

If there is a difficult conversation you need to have with someone or if you need the strength to make a difficult decision, bring the situation into your mind and pretend you are the Sovereign of the realm. Your role is to protect the vision and integrity of the land.

Make your decision or pronouncements in your mind and see how it feels.

Have that difficult conversation in your mind, see it resolved and visualize the other person feeling peaceful and happy.

When you are ready to move into action, open your eyes feeling empowered, triumphant, wise and calm.

# Chapter 2: Memoir Mirror

*"Writers aren't exactly people... They're a whole bunch of people trying to be one person."*

**–F. Scott Fitzgerald**

Your business is the grounded vision of your highest self. And like the soul, your business has its own desires.

Within your brand exists the reflected + refracted pieces of *you— the many are the one.*

How you bring the invisible to visibility through your work is magical.

For this chapter we'll be diving underneath the surface of our stories to find gems to share with the world. We each have many faces to unmask.

I love looking at these other aspects as simply newly uncovered voices searching for a home. For in remembering and putting the chorus together, we spiral back to our centers.

We can't talk about memory, imagination or story without bringing in the archetype of Memory itself, the Greek Titaness Mnemosyne.

Mnemosyne, the personification of Memory and mother of the nine Muses, is credited with inventing language. Remembering is a creative, imaginative activity. The "facts" we remember are completely subjective. Ask one of your siblings about a profound or traumatic family moment you shared and I can guarantee you'll each have a different story to tell!

Memory and memoir are the flowing streams from which inspiration is born. Who hasn't sat next to a babbling brook and heard the voices of the nine Muses? Or the birds singing lulling us back to a time of innocence, grace and sweetness.

Wishing wells and holy springs are the homes of elementals, faes and guardian angels. If you've been to Celtic countries and seen pieces of cloth and ribbon tied to trees next to sacred springs and wells, you've seen the work of Mnemosyne. Think of Goddess Memory in this deeper, more complex way, instead of as simple memorization by rote.

The number of muses is significant as well. Nine is a Cosmic number related to the crone, hermit or mystical sage. It also represents the number of months that it takes to gestate a child in the womb. The nine Muses are tributaries that flow from the great river, Mother Mnemosyne.

Each Muse represents an aspect of preserving, embodying and expressing a memory:

- Calliope (Epic Poetry)
- Clio (History)
- Erato (Love Poetry)
- Euterpe (Music)
- Melpomene (Tragedy)
- Polyhymnia (Hymns)
- Terpsichore (Dance)
- Thalia (Comedy)
- Urania (Astronomy)

Mnemosyne, memory itself, is likened to the water element... in fact, initiates of the Orphic mysteries were directed to drink from a pool of water that was Mnemosyne, instead of from the river Lethe ("forgetfulness").

Water reflects, and clear or murky, can be seen through. Water refracts light like a mirror. When the sun hits the waves of the ocean, its light shatters into sparkling pieces, displaying unity in diversity.

Mirrors are physical representations of water in sacred esoteric magic, for example their use in scrying. Magical beings use bowls of water and mirrors to view the past, present and future. When they relax and focus their gaze gently on a bowl of water or a blacked out non-reflective mirror, oracular images appear. Likewise, as you work with your brand in this chapter, you will begin to see how it connects to both your memories of the past and its future incarnation. The brand reaches backwards as it stretches out in front of you, directing the course of your business.

Memoir is similar; it expresses a *telos*—a view of the future within the past and the past within the future. We can enter another's story through a shard of time, a splinter of their life. That miniscule piece tells us as much as if we had read their whole biography in chronological order. One moment can define a whole life experience.

Because we often see ourselves reflected back through other's stories, there is no more potent way learn about our inner life.

# Case Study: Michelle Ward

Quirky, loveable, off-the-wall, goofy and simply Amazeballs!

That's Michelle Ward, the When I Grow Up coach.

Like the actress she once was, she channels multiple archetypes with ease: the Divine Child, Champion of Creatives and Imagineers, as well as the Comic Muse (like Baubo who lifts Demeter out of her depression).

To help her clients figure out how to navigate from cubicle-doom to entrepreneurial freedom she channels her inner Nancy Drew, the brave, curious, girl detective, and Ramona Quimby, the super imaginative pre-teen who wishes to save her family and friends. (Remember the name Ramona… you'll read about her again at the end of the case study.)

Michelle's own debacle with a "career coach" set her on the path to help people figure out what they want to be when they grow up.

More than anything Michelle reminds us to embrace our "uniquity."

Her book, *The Declaration of You: How to Find it, Own it and Shout it From the Rooftops*, co-authored with Jessica Swift began as an eCourse back in 2011. Michelle and Jessica created a special character named Pierre François Frédéric to take the reader on the journey. He's even their mascot on Twitter who says things like, "I will be zee famous now that @jessicagswift & @WhenIGroUpCoach got zee book deal with @fwcraft ! Maybe I will meet zee Judge Judy?" *Tres magnifique, no?*

> *"Pierre François Frédéric is a Frenchman who used The Declaration of You (or, as he calls it, Zee Declaration of You) to discover his love of party hats, using animals for transportation, and brightly-colored attire. He has always been a wonderful lover and Judge Judy fan, and is making all the girls crazy by serenading*

*them with his singing voice and on the Twitter machine. You can also find him on the Facebook, eating many desserts at T. G. I. Friday's, and riding Jean-Luc Zee Pony."* (from *The Declaration of You* website)

She can't be compared to any other coach I know out there. She's zany, zesty, zealous and zephyrean. See Pierre? I too know many words that begin with *zee*.

Michelle's background in musical theatre brings another archetypal image to mind: the symbol of the dramatic arts as the masked faces, Comedy and Tragedy. The fullest expression of comedy must have a color of tragedy and vice versa.

In 2012 Michelle was diagnosed with breast cancer. At her young age, this was a big wake up call for many of us who gathered to rally around her. It was a scary time, an unwanted call from the Underworld. However, Michelle found a way to bring in the healing archetype of humor through writing and performing a comedic song, "I got boob cancer (a ditty)" on YouTube.

(It's amazeballs and you can find it here: www.youtube.com/watch?v=y7CD-UVyM3w)

Her follow up ditty was "I'm Gettin' New Boobs." She released it after her lumpectomy and a report came back from her doctor that the cancer had spread beyond the original lump. Now she was going a little further into the Underworld with chemotherapy and a double mastectomy. But, she was getting new (bigger) boobs, so there was a light at the end of the dark tunnel.

The young woman with the pink ukelele not only made us laugh through our tears, but was also able to raise $17,000 that year in the 2-day Avon Walk for Breast Cancer in New York.

Michelle has since appeared at Chris Guillebeau's World Domination Summit and has charmed audiences while teaching online.

Her 3-day workshop *Create Your Dream Career* on CreativeLive was the second highest viewed course in its category.

What inspires me most about Michelle's work is NOT her honesty, transparency, genius ideas and creative approach, but rather her indomitable spirit of fun in the face of adversity, change and fear.

She laughs at the notion of our economic recession, which she claims is "bullhonkey" and provides proof by profiling other entrepreneurs, such as myself, that have overcome their fear and created livelihoods that thrive and grow financially. At the same time Michelle doesn't trivialize feelings of sadness, defeat or discouragement. Rather she steps into her role of Champion to bolster others and help them get back on that horse again. As an entrepreneur she understands how debilitating the reality of failure can be and that we can't avoid falling on our asses from time to time. It's the nature of entrepreneurialism.

In 2014 she became mama bear to her gorgeous adopted daughter, Ramona… the same name of the character so formative to her own story of heroism: she teaches and embodies that to light the way for others we can't resist being our own unique, quirky selves.

# Unmask + Personify the Faces of Your Brand

*"Strike a pose."*

**–Madonna,** *Vogue*

Think Madonna. Angelina Jolie. Meryl Streep. They are actors who can wear many different masks naturally.

Each persona is valued equally as a unique expression of the self. For this chapter, I'd like you to meet three to seven different beings who are living inside your imagination. Some may wish to be a part of your mythic brand, or may have been incorporated already. If you don't reach seven or happen to meet more, no problem. The object of this imaginative play is to unmask the personas calling out to you for attention in the here and now.

Close your eyes and imagine that there is a hall with seven mirrors. Each mirror is decorated differently. Some are ornate and some plain, with every variation in between. Choose one that appeals to you and stand in front of it. See your reflection transform into a new face. Have a dialogue with this new face as if with an old friend.

**Seven figures that came forward for me the first time I did the exercise:**

1. Beautiful Elegant Young Woman. Saucy, sassy pants personality, singer for a rock band. Wants me to have a mermaid rock band and be in front! She likes being in the spotlight.

2. Naked Mermaid, named Sandrine, who's an erotica writer, who was once a stripper. Proud nymphomaniac.

3. Sword Wielding Warrior Woman, Freya-type. Wants to save other women and girls, keep them from being taken advantage of. Smells bullshit a mile away. Totally speaks her mind, no filters, tells it like it is.

4. Mystical Healer Woman who is very motherly and exudes wisdom. She said she's been with me for thousands of years. She's a solitary priestess and needs lots of quiet time.

5. Traveling Minstrel, Storyteller, Gypsy woman. Keeps small daggers in the garters on her thighs. She's a good gambler and loves games, especially when money is on the line.

6. Dolphin. He guides me to an underwater Atlantean world inside of a glistening bubble so I can breathe.

7. Wanderer Man. Maverick who travels alone but pines for romance in his life. Dark skin, long black hair, reminds me of the characters from Last of the Mohicans. Sexy! Great fighter who comes to the defense of any underdog and loves listening to his friends' stories.

# Dream Oracle + Vision: Yemaya and I

One night, when I was nineteen years old, I had a vivid, memorable dream. A beautiful and bountiful woman with long, luxurious hair and dark brown skin rose out of the ocean. She was smiling and laughing and dancing. She called to me in a language that I did not speak, but seemed to understand. Her identity was a mystery; nevertheless, the dream image was burned into my memory.

In the dream space, I knew I was in Brazil. The beach was serene, and behind me there was a vast rain forest of green trees with colorful birds and monkeys cavorting in the branches. Nineteen years later, in 2006, I finally made a pilgrimage to Salvador, Bahia, Brazil. The trip was designed as a three-month fieldwork study of Candomblé ritual drumming to immerse myself into the culture, music, and mythology of this particular place that had so haunted my psyche. It was both a spiritual homecoming and an intellectual blossoming.

During my fieldwork, a divination with cowrie shells, known in Brazil as *jogo de buzios* ("shell game"), revealed that I have two patron *orixás*: the ocean *orixá* Iemanjá, who was the woman in my dream, and the *orixá* of winds and change, known as Iansã. A *mãe-de-santo* ("mother of the saint," a Candomblé priestess) named Marinalva conducted the divination that connected me to the spiritual aspect of my research and the dream that made such a deep psychological mark on my life.

During the time period that I dreamed about Iemanjá, I was studying and practicing rhythms of the African Diaspora on percussion instruments derived from the Santeria and Candomblé religious traditions, particularly *congas*, *timbales* and *pandeiro* (a tambourine-like instrument). Years later, I discovered that the previous owner of my congas was a Macumba priest; he is also a well-known Brazilian percussionist named Laudir de Olivera.

Since I do not have any familial, genetic ties to Brazil or Africa, I asserted that perhaps Iemanjá connected with me through those specific drums as well as through the music and rhythms. These rhythms were in popular and Latin-jazz musical styles. The year was 1987, memorable because it marked my first initiation into the scholarly world—the commencement of my undergraduate studies in music.

Iemanjá, mother of most of the *orixás* and the second wife of Oxalá, is the universal mother, revered in Brazil as the mother who loves unconditionally. She is, after all, Omolu's adopted mother who takes him in after he is rejected by his own mother, Nanã.

Her domain extends from the sparkling reflective surface of the ocean, all the way down to its deep, obscure, cold depths.

Iemanjá is the quintessential Great Mother of Candomblé, beloved by a large majority of practitioners and non-practitioners alike in Brazil. She is celebrated in large *festas* on both December 8 and February 2, and is petitioned daily for fertility, financial abundance and help gaining a spouse.

The following meditation connects you to Yemaya and will allow you the chance to ask her for a wish to hold dear to your heart.

## Meditation Vision Journey to Visit the Undersea Palace of Yemaya

Move your consciousness down into your lower abdomen, your creative center. This is the entrance to your etheric body, governed by the element of water and the *orixá* Yemanja. You feel an ancient call to to dive deep into your watery realms, your dreams and desires. Feel your consciousness fully rooted in this area of creativity and power.

Someone is calling your name. The language is foreign, yet somehow you know that this is a call from the mystical realm. It is a call you cannot deny.

Feel your consciousness firmly placed in your primal creative power. Breathe deeply into your core.

You are standing on the edge of a vast ocean, the tide is high and foamy waves are crashing at your feet. The moon is full overhead and its reflection plays on the waves in silvery blue streaks.

You count seven waves coming towards the shore. One. Two. Three. Four. Five. Six.

And just beyond the 7th wave is a radiant woman, larger than any human, with dark brown skin gleaming in the moonlight. Streams of white gardenias and roses flow out all around her and dolphins and colorful fish playfully attend her.

As she floats closer and closer to you on the wave, you begin to make out her facial features, her hair and garments.

This is the great Yemaya, mother of all life, mother of all sea creatures, the matrix of our very existence. You kneel at her feet and feel the flood of love she is sending you enter into the creative womb center in your lower abdomen. This energy is pure light and flows up from your womb center to purify all of your chakras, organs and each of your cells. Yemaya is blessing your creativity and your sexuality.

She reaches out her hands to you, so much larger than your own, and when you clasp them they feel strong and protective. She pulls you into the water and smiles. She transforms herself into a beautiful white marble entranceway. Now there are two great pillars standing on either side of you. You hear her voice again.

"What do you most desire to create? What do you want to give birth to?"

Allow some time to ponder her question carefully because whatever you desire and ask for you will receive.

Once you have the answer, swim through the threshold and find yourself in Yemaya's underwater palace fashioned completely of glistening white and silver marble and stone. Corals decorate the walls in every shade of color imaginable.

The palace is a wonder to behold.

Begin to explore the rooms and halls of her palace.

Suddenly you hear drumming and singing in the distance; Yemaya is always in a state of celebration.

You follow the sound into a palatial ballroom, all white with mirrors made from the shiniest platinum. The domed ceiling is made entirely of blue lapis.

There must be hundreds of beings in this gigantic room and they step aside as you walk towards the center. You notice familiar faces of mentors, ancestors and even famous people you admire. All of them seem to be there to celebrate YOU and your accomplishments.

Yemaya now approaches in her smaller, human size and holds a beautiful mirror up for you to gaze in. A white sparkling mist begins to form in the mirror and you see images of yourself engaged in your creative projects and pursuits. You watch them take form and come into fruition.

The mirror returns to its normal reflective state and Yemaya takes you by the arm and promenades you around the great circle.

Each being present bows their head in reverence and gratitude. Your powerful, creative work has transformed you and the world for the better.

Take in and receive the applause, reverence, love, respect, admiration and gratitude bestowed upon you. Feel this energy like a power surge of bliss and joy coursing through your body, energizing and nourishing your soul.

Yemaya leads you through the palace and out the threshold between the two white pillars to return you safely back to the seashore. She blesses you with a gift, a symbolic object to bring with you into normal, everyday waking consciousness. The object will give you the hope and faith to sustain you as you birth your most beloved creative projects.

Thank her for her care, nurturing and protection. If you have questions, ask her now. She can guide you to take any right actions to see your projects through to completion. Return to her whenever you need guidance, encouragement or solace.

Say your farewell to Yemaya by kneeling down before her and touching your forehead to the sandy, wet earth at her feet. Now look at her and speak aloud or silently her salutation with heartfelt reverence: "Odo Iya, Odo Iya, Odo Iya."

Whatever you need she will provide, for she is the granter of wishes and she wants you to be live happily in a state of celebration.

Yemaya dematerializes into the white sea foam.

**Journaling Prompts:**

Describe your experiences while doing the meditation in as much detail as you can remember.

How can you take action on a dream/wish that Yemaya wants to grant you? What instructions did she give you? Or what does your intuition tell you the next steps are?

(The recorded meditation journey that you can follow along with is available by registering your name and email at www. ReturnToEnchantment.com)

# Athena: The Archetype of Vision + Wisdom

Athena's an Olympian goddess, the daughter of Zeus and Metis. The Greek word *metis* means "cunning and magical wisdom."

Her animal totem is the owl, the bird that can see into the darkness and knows exactly where to go and what to do. The wise owl can be connected to our intuitive wisdom, the insight that comes from within. I think it interesting that the third eye chakra is named *ajna* - which means "command." Our command center is this base of intuitive wisdom that comes from **the** authority, the Divine Source itself.

Serpents entwine both of Athena's lower arms, wrap around her upper arm and wrap around her waist like a belt. She has the face of Medusa on her aegis, over her heart chakra, and if you remember, Medusa's hair is made of snakes. Athena cursed Medusa for making love with Poseidon in her temple. Because we are dealing with a patriarchal mythology, Athena does nothing to punish Poseidon, who knew what he was doing and that their copulation in the temple was forbidden; Medusa was the most beautiful Amazon in the world and she was turned into a monster that could turn anyone who gazed upon her to stone.

Snake energy is transformational, shedding the skin, renewal, rebirth. And the symbol par excellence of the Great Mother, Divine Feminine.

Athena teaches us to be self-empowered, to be strategic, to be creative and inventive. To be bold and be ruled by our own authority.

# Interview: Tanya Geisler

*I love to talk about the archetypal resonance of the stories, characters, and archetypes and how we live them out in our lives and livelihood. And as you know, I'm particularly fascinated with entrepreneurs as the dreamers, mystics, and messengers of our time. And today I am delighted and honored to highlight a messenger who empowers so many through her words and her work, and that is Miss Tanya Geisler. I adore Tanya.*

*One of the first blog posts I saw of her's was basically adoration of her daughter. It was wishes for her 8th birthday and she continues to write these inspiring, beautiful poetry blessings about her daughter on her blog.*

*Tanya is the Step Into Your Starring Role creatrix and coach. She has created many offerings to assist entrepreneurs in engineering and manifesting their intentional, meaningful and joyous lives.*

*Those are all her words and what she's bringing in.*

*She is sassy, bold, funny, and she won't let you slip because she really is here to help you midwife the biggest self that you can bring to the table right now.*

Wooohooo! My goodness. I think I'm going to need a printout of that, my friend. That was awesome. Thank you. I feel very welcomed and seen.

*I want to talk about your connection to Athena. One of the things that I do before I interview my wonderful folks, is send them questions about their favorite mythological characters, stories, scenes from stories, archetypes. And they send me back a list.*

*Athena was one that really jumped out at me, because of your work around authority and the imposter complex—the subject of your gorgeous and inspiring TED Talk I watched on your website.*

So, it's a big conversation. Well, let me just say this too, right? You know, in that list, I also had Anne Shirley, Anne of Green Gables. I suspect there's some great thesis in there that could probably join the two at the hip—their passion for their wisdom, their courage, their inspiration. So I think there are probably some connections there too, but I'm not surprised that Athena caught your eye.

*I feel like your work really asks two questions: What is the command center? What is the center of authority?*

Those questions are very central to the work. What is your authority? How can you claim your authority? We are so wrought with the gaucheness, the too much-ness of owning and claiming our expertise, our authority; we default so quickly to not ready yet. Don't know enough, don't have the degrees, don't have the credentials, don't have… *don't have, don't have. Not ready yet.*

Central to the work that I do, is absolutely having people step into the starring role of their lives and their work, which is really another way of saying stepping into their authority.

How can you even talk about Athena in a twenty-minute conversation? When I think of her, it's about strategy. Right? It's not about winning by force. It's about being intelligent and strategic, about how we want to have it play out. Whatever the *it* is. The process of stepping into authority is a very strategic process.

*Can you tell us a little bit more about the process?*

It really starts with our own decision to strive. Where is it that we want to be? What is truly central to our authority? What is it that we want, that we know? That we are an authority in, but we haven't claimed it yet. Making that decision is truly the very first step. And so all of a sudden, all sorts of things start to show up, "No! You can't have it be that way," all of those self-limiting beliefs. You need to face all of them head-on.

What are the realistic objections that show up for you as you decide to strive? And what are the unrealistic objections? Who are the saboteurs? Who are the inner critics? So, really meeting them head-on, dealing with what needs to be dealt with and dispensing the rest. That is clearly huge process that can take a significant amount of time.

Meeting those critics and then going to a place of bolstering your authority thesis: What is it that you do know? What have you achieved, accomplished? This is about rooting into the truth about you. I have a very strong foundational belief that people, *your people*, really want you to succeed.

Part of this is now assembling the cast. What are the gaps where you will need support as your fully step into your authority, step into your starring role? Then it's putting in the time and doing the work. But I think it's really more like, what are the 10,000 choices that you need to make to continue down the path.

And then celebrating! Celebrating what we've achieved is something that is truly undervalued. It's just had really bad PR. Celebration. It's light, it's fluffy, but it also conditions us to be able to accept more.

I think of the whole process, this strategy, as an upward spiral and that's what we continue to do. We continue to decide to strive.

*I love that you teach the strategy of joy so it ties into that celebration piece. There's something about joy that impacts the experiences in a different way.*

We start the **Step into Your Starring Role** program with an exercise called *Your Brand of Joy* because "joy" can be a real trigger word for some people. An expression of joy, the conditions of my joy, are actually more important than the word that I have used to associate. For me it's about **connection** and **generosity** and **gratitude**. When I have those three tenets, when they're alive and well, that's when I'm in joy. But I've realized that what I call joy, my friend Julie calls love. What she calls love and I call joy, my husband calls success. So, knowing your own brand of joy is absolutely paramount to deciding to strive.

*Athena energy is very creative. Before she was associated more with the patriarchal myths, you know the Olympians and Zeus, she was revered in Minoan, Crete. She was the patroness of pottery; she taught the people how to make pottery from clay. And weaving. If you look at her images and statues, of pre and post-patriarchal Athena, she is covered with serpents. Athena's all about snake energy. That transformation of renewal, rebirth.*

When you were talking about the snakes, I immediately went to the caduceus, you know the like ancient symbol of science—medicine, I think it is. That sort of winding spiraling energy of this snake going up the caduceus. That is the true representation of the work that I feel like I'm doing here. With the people that I'm working with one-on-one and in my group programs, we continue to move up this spiral.

I created my program **Board of Your Life** out of necessity; it was something that I needed. It was a spiral of positive energy that got me hooked. **Board of Your Life** is very tribal and ancient in its expression. Imagine that somebody in the tribe loses their medicine. The whole tribe is out of whack until that person gets their medicine back.

Somebody has a desire to make a shift, to make a change. They bring in people from their own life who know them in different capacities, who reflect what they see in that person. It behooves all of them to help that person reclaim their medicine. Everybody walks away from this experience saying hey, when am I really powerful? When am I on purpose? When am I living my most joyous experience? There's that spiraling again.

*The crime of outshining is something you have written about on your blog.*

Gay Hendricks in the *Big Leap* talks about it. We have all had the experience of outshining. Underneath most of our fears is the fear of being alone. We don't want to be too bright and sure as heck don't want to be too dark, because either way we drive people away. This is a belief that we have.

There's vulnerability in the celebration, because it amplifies the light and the dark. I take celebration really seriously; it's a huge edge for most of us. We're just terrified of having our shadowplace, our worries exposed, our flaws, our fears. But we're also terrified of having our joys exposed, our light, our shine. It could be part of our upbringing, being told good girls don't brag.

*Am I going to be alone in my party hat? I know my friends can be with me in my tears but will they also stand with me in my joy.*

Who are the women or men who see our shine and love it for what it is?

This is what I refer to as assembling your cast. Who are the people that will be with you in shine? I truly believe that your people want you to succeed.

*Stepping into your starring role is your more-ness and it's inclusive.*

Part of what I so deeply appreciate about the experience of stepping into a starring role, is that after we take the stage, there's so much more room on that stage for others. You know? When you look at some real superstars, you can see how they make space for others and how they inspire the same in others. And truly, my people have deep desires to be of service and they know that by modeling this, they're going to be reaching more people and invoking the same in them.

# Write a Mini-Memoir to Use for Your "About" Page or Any Bio

Write one to three character sketches of your favorite personas. Alex Franzen calls this a "Once Upon a Time" Bio:

Jot down the first four ages you can think of followed by "Today." For example:

**Age 5:**

**Age 12:**

**Age 17:**

**Age 27:**

**Today:**

Ink out who you were, at each chronological demarcation.

- **What were you doing with your life, at that time?**
- **What were your most urgent priorities?**
- **Who did you want to become?**
- **Which obstacles were stomping across your pathway?**
- **What mattered? What didn't?**
- And how about... right now? Who are you becoming?

*(You will find many great writing prompts on Alexandra's website. The link is in the Resources chapter of this book.)*

# Exploration: Acting "As If"

**Become Madonna, Angelina or Meryl for a day...**

Spend **one** day pretending to be one of the characters you met in the mirror meditation.

Dress the part and order coffee or breakfast as him or her. Let that persona answer your phone, emails. Write a newsletter or blog post.

How does the outside world meet this persona?

How do you feel to be wearing their shoes?

# Meditation + Breathwork

**Focus**: 6th Chakra

**Sanskrit**: Ajna, To Perceive, Command

**Associations**: Owl, Indigo to Turquoise Blue, Intuition, Seeing in the Dark and Wisdom

**Planet**: Moon

**Day of the Week**: Monday

**Archetypes**: High Priestess, Sorcerer, Mystic, Athena, Sulis, Merlin, Sage, Shaman, Witch

Ajna is also known as the Brow Chakra, the seat of our intuitive vision and psychic abilities.

Ajna is highly active on Monday, the day connected to the moon. The owl and the dolphin are often associated with our mystical center because the owl can see in the dark and dolphins send messages telepathically through touch. They have sophisticated language skills but are not as reliant on them as we are, their human brothers and sisters.

When your Brow chakra is clear you have access to Divine downloads 24/7. Continue to purify and strengthen your 6th chakra and you'll never have a creative dry spell!

Step 1: Begin to inhale slowly in a count of four through the petals of your brow chakra.

Step 2: Hold the breath for four counts, allowing the indigo blue light to expand and spread.

Step 3: When you exhale, breathe the indigo blue light out through the petals of your brow chakra into your aura, which surrounds your entire body.

Step 4: Hold your breath for four counts visualizing the indigo blue-colored light infusing your aura and bathing every cell of your body.

Repeat the pattern beginning with step 1 at least three more times.

To close the practice, breathe in Cosmic energy through your crown chakra and send the light down through your spinal column, then ground this energy deep into the heart of mother earth.

## Body Prayer

This simple body prayer movement sequence will help you embody the energy of Vision.

Stand in front of a mirror and place your hands together in *anjali mudra* (prayer position) in front of your heart.

Spend 5 minutes gazing into your own eyes.

Fully appreciate every feature on your face. Smile at yourself.

### Journaling Prompts:

What do you see in your own eyes? What stories do they have to tell?

How does it feel to stare into your own eyes each morning?

# Chapter 3: Midrash Movement

*"Imagination is everything. It is the preview of life's coming attractions."*

**–Albert Einstein**

This chapter is designed to help you discover and formulate the imaginative truths of your brand.

We often believe that imagination and its luminescent, magical world are not real.

"Just figments of the imagination…" is what we're told when we tell someone that we've seen a fairy or an angel or a ghost. The imaginal is most definitely real and the more you engage it through daydream, ritual and creative projects the more it will show its glimmering self to you.

The easiest and most pleasurable way to engage the imagination is to revise the stories and myths that have captured and delighted you. The official name of this storytelling method is *midrash*.

Midrash is a form of rabbinic literature that reinterprets ancient scriptures to address troubling omissions or gaps in stories. We will use a similar approach to our brand stories.

You'll begin dreaming your Mythic Brand forward… even though you may be accessing stories from the past, you'll begin to see even more clearly how you are living these truths today.

By playing with the truths of your brand, you will find new paths, opportunities and ways to move your business' story into the future.

Ultimately, you have the power to decide what is true for you NOW. Flushing out past beliefs, or truths that were adopted from the family and society you were born to, will help bring consciousness around self-limiting thoughts and habits. After exploring the stories you're telling, you'll gain a clear picture of ways you've given away your power.

What is truth for one person will be folly to another. Remain strong in your integrity and at the same time keep an open mind. Beginners mind will refresh your outlook and help you fall in love with your brand ALL over again.

It's time to know and to speak your truth.

# Self-Expression in Brand Storying, aka Midrashing Your Brand

Let's focus on the unique story you are channeling through your brand.

What keeps you awake at night? What troubling doubts do you face as you write the sales page or email for your next offering?

To release doubts and dissolve stumbling blocks, begin by looking at the deepest truths that your brand is striving to communicate. If you've been feeling stagnant in a particular area of branding or business building, this approach will help you.

Midrash is a Hebrew term that literally means "to study" and "to go in pursuit of." The form emerged as a calling to engage deeply with a scripture through meditation and application.

Let's apply this approach to your own myths to find what needs to be opened up, explored further and made relevant to who you are now and your present circumstances.

You'll find that "midrashing your brand" is a pleasurable and playful way to reimagine your stories.

1. I encourage you to read novels or watch some films that are considered popular midrash. A few examples that are high on my recommendation list are: *The Mists of Avalon*, *The Red Tent*, *The Passion of Mary Magdalene* (for that matter, everything in the Maeve Chronicle series).

   **Also check out any fun retellings of old stories and myths:**

   • Sherlock (TV) - Adventures of Sherlock Holmes

   • O' Brother, Where Art Thou (Film) - The Odyssey

- Bridget Jones' Diary (Novel, Film) - Pride and Prejudice

- My Fair Lady (Musical Theatre, Film) - Pygmalion

- Ever After (Film) - Cinderella

- 10 Things I Hate About You (Film) - Taming of the Shrew

- West Side Story (Musical Theatre, Film) - Romeo and Juliet

- The Truth About Cats & Dogs (Film) - Cyrano de Bergerac

2. What stories about your Mythic Brand feel like an old, outworn recording that plays over and over? Do you recognize the problems and a potential refreshing revisioning to them? You may just change parts of the stories or decide that they need to be replaced 100%!

3. What would it look like if every day held the potential for a Pleasure Party at your Mythic Brand headquarters?

4. As the CEO of your Mythic Brand, write a memo to all of your employees asking them to make pleasure + play a number 1 priority + tell them WHY. Give them suggestions HOW to do it. I feel a new kind of brand manifesto comin' on!

5. If your Mythic Brand were a song, what would be it's title? What style of music? Describe it as fully as you can, even include some lyrics if something begins to form.

# Case Study: Alexandra Franzen, Anti-Heroine and Unicorn

*"When you speak, sing, write, dance, muse & move to the beat of your invisible freak-drum—impeccably, messily, off-key or onpoint— you grant heroic permission. You crack every ceiling. You strike awe & hit home. You move people to share their own incandescent awesomery."*

## –Alexandra Franzen

Like the unicorn, her mythical ally and soulmate, Alexandra possesses healing and truth-revealing talents. She is no mere copywriter, scribe or marketing genius. She is a purveyor of "once or twice in a lifetime" soul transforming experiences.

In a Skype interview with Alexandra, I learned why positioning yourself like Placido Domingo (think one night of special engagements, not multitudes of small appearances here and there) can help you become a much sought-after entrepreneur with a yearlong waiting list. This interview is included in Chapter 7. Besides her incredible depth as an author and teacher, Alexandra is a lightning-fast writer, unmatched by any other copywriters I've ever worked with.

**Alexandra the Healer.**

In myth, and particularly medieval art, the unicorn is depicted next to a virgin maiden and a fruit tree. Purity and fertility are the two oppositions brought together in this visual motif.

A parallel theme is the unicorn on a virgin's lap as it's being pierced by a hunter's spear. The maiden is trying to stop the murder of the unicorn, even as the creature itself is passively sitting in a sacrificial stance.

In this scene, the unicorn is lured by the purity of the maiden where it lies down to be killed. The Christian associations are clearly illustrated here, yet I want to swim in a slightly different direction.

## Magic streams from innocence.

If you think about your own childhood daydreams, don't you feel nostalgic for that magical world? This paradisiacal state ends with the death of our imagination. The loss of our childhood dreams are tantamount to the loss of soul.

When you work with her in a workshop or read her blog, you'll find that one of the most important aspects of Alexandra's work is soul recovery (she might refer to it as figuring out *who you are becoming*).

Through her work, her clients get a deep sense that the seed of their future selves has been there all along waiting to be remembered.

## Alexandra the Great.

"I am a messenger of ease, in an un-easy world."

While most medieval and modern renditions of the unicorn emphasize it's magical and healing qualities (its horn could heal disease and neutralize poison), the unicorn was also considered a ferocious creature that would skewer anyone that got too close.

One description of the unicorn appears in a vision of the prophet Daniel (Book of Daniel, 8:5):

> "And as I was considering, behold, a he-goat came from the west over the face of the whole earth, and touched not the ground: and the goat had a notable horn between his eyes...

Many scholars believe this prophecy is a reference to Alexander the Great, an unstoppable conqueror who may have ridden a unicorn into battle, and at the very least, had the strong, untamable aspects that were associated with the unicorn." (Diana Peterfreund)

The Alexandra I've come to know and love is not only a polished, professional author, speaker and teacher, she's an anti-heroine.

## So, what is an Anti-Hero/ine?

> By definition the anti-hero is not the opposite of the hero, rather it is a character "who may be an outlaw or a villain from the point of view of society, but with whom the audience is basically in sympathy" (Vogler, *The Writer's Journey*, 34).

Anti-heroes are often my favorite characters in films: think Doc Holliday, Han Solo, Robin Hood, Catwoman and Scarlett O'Hara. Even Lady Gaga has the flavor of the anti-heroine.

Alexandra has not gotten to where she is today by being conventional. She's strong, sexy, gentle, soft-spoken, persuasive, elegant, punky, gorgeous, earthy, healing, lyrical heavenly, tough, loving and whacky. She's just so... herself. Imagine that? And, she changes the world one entrepreneur, blog post, book and workshop at a time.

"That's why my gifts are valuable. Not because I had to 'fight' for them—but because they are rare. Because they are graceful.

Because they come easy."

Alexandra is anything but conventional and her approach to work has helped to revitalize many a solopreneur.

The "shoulds" around how to be a "successful" entrepreneur can leave so many of us overwhelmed and burned out. Mere husks of our true selves as we strive for a "model" of perfection that we see outside of ourselves.

"My top three idols are Mr. Rogers, Oscar Wilde & RuPaul. Basically, I want Mr. Rogers' compassion (and infinite cardigan collection), Oscar Wilde's wit & whimsy, and RuPaul's salacious self-confidence. (I'm getting there.)" She says.

Alexandra's anti-struggle, but not anti-suffering, at least in the sense that in letting go of our ego and surrendering to our highest purpose (and best creative rhythm)—suffering tempers and softens the soul. So we can break false molds we've been latching onto and adopt our own instead. They have been there all along. They are ours.

"Pay close attention to the times that you shine, without breaking a sweat. Pick up on the timing—and tender, tiny details."

While taking her workshop, Write Yourself Into Motion, I realized my creative rhythm and that how I wanted to work was completely different from how I was working day-to-day.

I crave in-person, personal contact, especially after working exclusively online and over the phone for the past two years. And, I need to work by the ocean and in water as much as possible in beautiful surroundings. (I'm a mermaid after all!)

Now that you have the anti-model for being a wildly passionate and fulfilled (forget "successful") entrepreneur, go forth and jam to your rhythm.

The world is waiting!

*(Alexandra's case study first appeared on Rebelle Society.)*

# Truth-Telling Your Brand

*"There is no such thing as a true tale. Truth has many faces and the truth is like to the old road to Avalon; it depends on your own will, and your own thoughts, whither the road will take you."*

**–Marion Zimmer Bradley,** *The Mists of Avalon*

Over the next two weeks, particularly after you've loosened up through a relaxation session with your throat chakra breathing (instructions in the Meditation + Breathwork section), sit down to journal for five minutes on the following prompt:

**"The truth of my brand is…"**

That's it. A simple jam for five minutes each day if you can swing it. Begin to notice where you are going with the prompt. Are there any truths that come up repeatedly more than others?

Here are my truths from my first go at the exercise:

*The truth of my brand is that it is based on generosity.*

*… that it is mutually beneficial for me and others.*

*… that it's about loving my audience.*

*… that it's about being true to the images being birthed through the psyche.*

*… I want to serve thousands of entrepreneurs.*

*… I want to have freedom.*

I can break these down into one to five word value statements:

- Generosity
- Mutually Beneficial
- Loving My Audience

- Being Truthful
- Authentic
- Transformation
- In Service to Thousands
- Freedom

When you tire of that prompt here are some others:

**"The truth of my [type of offering], [name of offering], is…"**

{Example: The truth of my book, *Return to Enchantment*, is to explore approaches to mythologizing your brand without concretizing and weakening its images."}

**"The truth of my SDC [supernaturally designed client=ideal client] is…"**

**"If the truth of my brand is [truth #2, let's say], then…"**

**"If the truth of my customer is [truth of your SDC, let's say], then…"**

**"If the world was about to be destroyed by a comet, my brand would [help, demonstrate, protect, preserve]…"**

**"My brand is vital to the world because…"**

# Interview: Demi Mermaid Priestess

*When did you become the Mermaid Priestess that you are today?*

I feel like my mermaid priestess-ness has slowly been coming together over the last six years, since I turned 20. It's like I strip back a layer and there are mermaids there, and the more I discover about myself and the more deeply I fall into my spirituality, the more mermaids there are. I really feel that I am a Mermaid Priestess—mermaids are all about strength and self-love, sovereignty and following your own star, whatever that might be, and that really resonates with me as a total dreamchaser.

*How did you receive the siren call?*

For me, it's always been mermaids. I rediscovered Mermaids in university when researching folklore stories for my art degree, after a childhood of being completely obsessed with *The Little Mermaid*.

The stories and the lore of the mermaids really spoke to me. They are such a union of light and shadow, of being exactly who they are and not giving a fuck if they are contradictory or too emotional or wild or not what someone wants. I've been a spiritual peep since I was about 12, discovering the Goddess through witchcraft, and Mermaids to me are just the ultimate expression of the Divine Feminine—they are sovereignty, self love, and pure *badacity* rolled into one.

I just can't even tell you how excited and worked up I get about the Mermaid Archetype. Eeep!

*Favorite mermaids and myths and stories?*

Of course, Disney's *The Little Mermaid* has been a huge influence on everything that happened after I was seven years old. I think it's the chasing a dream no matter what aspect of it that got me—Ariel always wanted to go to the human world no matter what, Prince Eric was just an excuse really. She would have done it anyway.

There are so many stories I love, but the thing I love most about them is that Mermaids were used as a way to demonize womenkind, so were given all the "bad bits" of woman—vanity, jealousy, insatiable sexual appetite (wink wink!), danger, mystery, changeable natures, sexiness - and were used to show how scary and evil and powerful women were. Isn't that just so cool?

Mermaids show the raw wild realness of women, and represent a true, whole, unedited feminine essence—with all the good stuff and the shitty stuff.

And you know what? Mermaids are always cool with who they are, no matter what they do or how evil they are, and that's what made them so terrifying in the past—a woman who knows she is great just as she is and respects herself, no matter what.

***You are a dancer, writer and priestess mermaid... tell us more about your work and how you use the mermaid myth in your marketing.***

I gave up all pretence of living a normal human 9-to-5ish life just over a year ago. It's not for me, and it never was. I'm pretty much all mermaids all the time.

I actually work as a professional mermaid, as in, it's my job to rock up and be a mermaid to entertain people, and I am a co- founder of the top UK mermaid performance company Merlesque (our site lives at www.realmermaids.co.uk). We like to use all the mermaid aspects possible, which means you can see us enchanting children at birthday parties by day, and singing dirty songs about drowning men, in burlesque clubs at night.

My other main job is belly dance teacher and dance performer— if a mermaid gave up swimming for walking, I am pretty sure it would be because she wanted to dance!

Spirituality has always been a huge part of my life, and I totally fell in love with the Divine Feminine in my early teens. I run

a spiritual blog and biz called **Rockstar Priestess** over at www.
priestesstraining.com where I talk a lot about my priestess training,
the Goddess, Priestessing, and a whole bunch about Mermaids too
of course.

I paint portraits of people as mermaids, for people who want more
mermaid magic in their lives and who, on some level, WISH they
could leave the human world behind and be free as a mermaid
forever.

In every professional circle I am known as The Mermaid. That's
how people get introduced to me now—"Have you met Demi?
She's a mermaid..."

I'm working on a big project about Mermaids on my Priestess site
too - it's early stages now but it's all about changing your life using
the inspiration of mermaids! It's based on what is working for me
in my life and is currently called *Fuck This: I Want to Be a Mermaid*,
because I am a swear bear by nature and because mermaids have
the most fun. I am hoping to launch it sometime in the New Year.
I am REALLY excited about it!

Mermaids are playing an ever larger part in my life and especially
in my spirituality. I am going to be talking a LOT about mermaid
inspiration and spirituality over on Rockstar Priestess over the
next few months, so join me if you like priestesses and mermaids,
because that's all I write about really.

# Meditation + Breathwork

**Focus**: 5th Chakra

**Sanskrit**: Vishuddha, Purification

**Associations**: Sound, Voice, Speaking Your Truth, Communication, Writing, Integrity, Music, Rhythm, Whale, Dolphin and Turquoise Blue

**Planet**: Mercury

**Day of the Week**: Wednesday

**Archetypes**: Hermes/Mercury, Sarasvati, Ganesha, Vac, Oya

This chakra is located at the throat and is the seat of self-expression and creativity.

It has the power to transmute poison into nectar, and to purify negative thoughts and emotions through the knowledge of truth.

Step 1: Inhale slowly in a count of four through the petals of your throat chakra.

Step 2: Hold the breath for four counts, allowing the turquoise blue light to expand and spread.

Step 3: When you exhale, breathe the turquoise blue light out through the petals of your throat chakra into your aura, which surrounds your entire body.

Step 4: Hold your breath for four counts visualizing the turquoise blue-colored light infusing your aura and bathing every cell of your body.

Repeat the pattern beginning with Step 1 at least three more times.

To close the practice, breathe in Cosmic energy through your crown chakra and send the light down through your spinal column, then ground this energy deep into the heart of mother earth.

## Body Prayer

This simple body prayer meditation sequence will help you sink into the energies of communication + purification. It is in the silence that the longings of our hearts can bubble up to the surface to be expressed through the arts and language.

Sit upright or lie down flat on your back. Place one or both hands over your throat chakra. Close your eyes and be in the silence.

Imagine you are a whale or dolphin swimming in the deep, vast ocean. Soak in the serenity of your surroundings.

Begin to hum notes that vibrate your chest and nasal cavity and feel the reverberations reach down into the rest of your body. Allow them to massage relaxation into every muscle, releasing tension and letting go of pain.

To enhance your experience, play the sounds of whales and dolphins. You can find all sorts of great ambient sounds using whale and dolphin song on YouTube.

When you are complete, get out your journal and do the truth telling your brand exercise, or simply ask yourself, "What does my heart desire to express right now?"

(A recorded meditation journey for you to follow along with is available by registering your name and email at www. ReturnToEnchantment.com)

# Chapter 4: Waters of Aphrodite

*"I was born with my mouth open...*
*entering this juicy world*
*of peaches and lemons and ripe sun*
*and the pink and secret flesh of women,*
*this world where dinner is in the breath*
*of the subtle desert,*
*in the spices of the distant sea*
*which late at night drift over sleep.*
*I was born somewhere between the brain and the pomegranate,*
*with a tongue tasting the delicious textures*
*of hair and hands and eyes;*
*I was born out of the heart stew,*
*out of the infinite bed, to walk upon*
*this infinite earth."*

*–Eating the World* **by James Tipton**

**Welcome to the sensual delights of Aphrodite.**

At this point in our wonder journey together, we dip into Aphrodite's sacred pool of pleasure and initiation.

Aphrodite is an ancient Greek goddess who rules over sensuality, beauty, pleasure and procreation. Born in Cyprus, she arose naked from the sea foam, as a fully matured woman.

Why a chapter on pleasure and sensuality in a branding book?

First, a majority of my clients maintain that as we work on their branding, issues of vulnerability arise around their sensuality and sexuality. They notice that inhibitions they feel in bed with their lover or spouse are reflected in their inhibitions around creating a visible and enticing brand.

Many of us in westernized culture are endeavoring to overcome the inhibitions and taboos around sensuality and sexuality, physically experiencing + expressing pleasure.

The voices in our heads still echo the Puritanical morals that are part of the foundations of our society: sexuality and sensuality are still considered bad, ugly, evil, dirty, unclean.

If we can't let go and allow our sensual and sexual aspects to be expressed, we also can't fully shine in our wholeness.

# The Tale of Psyche + Eros

## (aka Cupid + Psyche)

My abbreviated version taken from Apuleius, 2nd Century AD, "The Golden Ass."

Once upon a time, in a rich and abundant kingdom there lived a king and queen.

They had three beautiful daughters. The youngest was so breathtakingly beautiful that words can't even describe her.

Psyche's famed beauty spread over countries even! People went on pilgrimages to view this living Goddess of Love. Meanwhile, Aphrodite's temples in Cyprus were empty and silent.

Aphrodite, the true Goddess of Love, grew jealous and vengeful for being upstaged by a human. She instructed her son Eros ("eros" is the Greek term for *romantic or intimate love*) to go to Psyche and shoot her with one of his arrows to make her fall in love with a man of ill repute. This would surely bring her to ruin and despair.

What Psyche pined for was a man who would truly love her, as herself, not as a goddess. Men in general were so hypnotized by her beauty that they didn't even want to court her!

We're going to jump further into the story: Psyche's father visits the oracle of Apollo, who informs the king that Psyche is to marry a monstrous creature. They must dress her for a wedding then abandon her to this rock at the top of a mountain where her new husband will claim her.

So, after they leave Psyche at the top of the mountain, a strong wind comes along and carries her to a sumptuous palace—obviously created by an immortal. It is the palace of Eros, himself. Psyche is cared for as if she were a queen, by invisible people. She hears their voices and feels their unseen hands undressing her, bathing her and dressing her again.

Finally, in her bed for the first night, her new husband (who is invisible as well) takes her in his arms and makes love to her. She is happy to finally be intimate with a man, but feels strangely lonely because all of the people around her are invisible.

Eros flies off each morning only to return to her at night. He warns Psyche that if she ever looks upon him he will disappear from her forever.

Psyche tells him that she loves him as much as her own soul. She calls him, "soul of my soul."

Psyche's sisters visit her at the palace. Seeing the floors made of gold and inlaid gems, they become poisoned by jealousy and envy. They go back and encourage Psyche to look at her husband by the light of an oil lamp, while he's sleeping. They tell her to take a sharp carving knife to stab him and kill him in his sleep.

Naively and innocently she follows her sisters' instructions and betrays Eros. She sees him lying asleep and she touches one of his arrows. It pierces her skin and she is overcome by an even deeper love—seeing his beautiful body laying there in bed, his handsome face. A drop of oil leaks from the lamp and burns him. He wakens abruptly and flies away angrily, repeating his promise of doom— that they can never see each other again.

Lovesick and suicidal, Psyche takes bitter revenge on her sisters

… they both die horrible deaths.

We are nearing the end of the story. Our heroine Psyche must face the wrath of Aphrodite, who's really pissed off now. Psyche implores her, saying that she will do anything to win back the heart of her beloved.

At this point, Aphrodite becomes Psyche's initiatrix. She gives Psyche four impossible tasks to complete:

1. Sort a huge pile of seeds.

2. Retrieve the Golden Fleece.

3. Fill a flask from the water that flows from the River Styx.

4. Return from the Underworld with a box of Persephone's beauty ointment.

With each task Psyche cries bitterly, for she is surely fated to fail. These are not tasks designed for a mere mortal after all! But, each time she faces certain death, a creature appears and gives her supernatural aid to complete the task. Then finally her Allies appear—a hoard of ants and the nature god Pan come to her aid. Even Zeus, chief of the gods sends his royal eagle to help her.

Aphrodite is truly ready to send Psyche to Hades, the place from which no mortal can return. Psyche's final task is to refill Aphrodite's jar of beauty cream, supplied by Persephone, Queen of the Dead. A trip to the Underworld is the classic part of all hero/ heroine's journeys. To face death is the biggest threat and challenge. And, when we take this beautiful tale for it's symbolic wealth, we know that death equals change and transformation. (A parallel to our thread of descending to the Underworld with Inanna.)

Returning triumphantly from the lower worlds with the box of beauty cream, Psyche allows her curiosity to get the best of her. She opens the box and falls into a deep, deathlike sleep.

Unable to stay away from his beloved and now fully recovered from the oil burn that nearly killed him, Eros flies across the land searching for Psyche. When he finds her, he sweeps the beauty mist or cream back into the box and instructs her to take it to his mother. Meanwhile he goes to beseech Zeus to allow him to marry Psyche. Zeus turns Psyche immortal so she can finally legitimately be married to Eros.

I love that at the end of the story, she has a daughter she names Voluptas, which means pleasure or bliss.

**The union of Love and the Soul begets Pleasure!**

Bliss is our true path and pleasure is our birthright as human beings. I truly believe that. Creating a livelihood should be no different. Bliss and pleasure are the results of our labors, just as they were the result of Psyche's trials.

The Greek name for Eros and Psyche's daughter Voluptas is *Hedone*. Hēdonē is an English transliteration of a Greek word meaning pleasure, and is the root of the English word "hedonism". In the philosophy of Epicurus, *hēdonē* was the quest for pleasure that could have only good consequences.

*Enlightened entrepreneurship is a quest for pleasure and bliss that has only good consequences.*

# Case Study: Helen Hodgson

One of my favorite clients Helen Hodgson has a brand that is permeated through and through with the Aphrodite archetype. Her mobile spa business Serve the Goddess (www.servethegoddess.com) was birthed in 2000 when Helen realized how many women there are who do not take care of themselves, women who put everyone else's needs first. This saddened her deeply. She remembered never seeing her own mother, a registered nurse, nurture herself. Following in her mother's footsteps, Helen found herself exhausted. Helen, determined put self-nurturing at the top of her to-do list, is now a "tireless" advocate, encouraging women everywhere to connect to their deep feminine core as a source of soul nourishment.

*"I believe every woman is born with a big, radiant mission. She may be a mother + homemaker, a visionary & artist, a nurse, a therapist or in any service capacity… or even a corporate CEO. And no matter what form her mission takes, she is worthy of love, reverence, time for self-reflection and deep relaxation. To be immersed in her own remarkable & unique essence. We're all worthy of self love and reverence.*

*So often in my work as a mobile spa owner and director, I see intelligent, loving and deserving women who are at their breaking point: many have crashed and burned before they even consider scheduling just one hour to themselves! The imbalances of a stressful life are felt throughout the whole being—body, mind and spirit. Our culture glorifies being "busy" and doing-ness. This just feels and sounds harsh to me. When a woman uses busyness as an excuse to put aside her own precious needs and desires, it saddens me. Deeply.*

*I created A Day in the Life series of retreats just for these women. My women.*

*Because I also believe we are all connected to a lineage of Sacred Feminine power; a power told in the ancient mythologies and stories of the Greek Goddesses. Maybe you have forgotten the stories. Maybe you have forgotten how to love and care for your body and soul. Through a sacred retreat, a vacation away from your day-to-day life, you will begin to remember."*

Besides her daily work with **Serve the Goddess mobile spa**, Helen offers retreats and workshops for women to renew, rejuvenate and tap into the healing archetypes of the **Greek goddesses: Aphrodite, Demeter, Athena, Persephone and Artemis.**

When Helen and I met in July 2013, we immediately connected. She scheduled a full day PLUNGE with me that summer. (The PLUNGE is one of my signature services; you can find it on www. krisoster.com.)

I knew I was in the presence of Aphrodite when I emailed her to find out where we could meet in person. She suggested we spend the day at her favorite resort **Terranea** in Rancho Palos Verdes, CA.

Ummmmm, wooottt?? Hell yeah!

**"This is a woman who knows how to pleasure herself and get things done," I thought to myself.**

After a full day of masterminding mind-blowing retreats and a bevy of new service packages based on her work with the Greek goddess archetypes (by the way, she has a line of sacred anointing oils too), we enjoyed lunch and a delicious beach ritual to seal in her renewed business and brand vision.

She was glowing and I was excited to get back home and begin crafting her new marketing + branding.

Just after I sent her some of my ideas, she emailed me this gorgeous testimonial letter:

*"I first met Kris when she was the guest speaker at the Goddess Collective in LA and she had me at Ph.D in Mythological Studies.*

*One week later I signed up for The PLUNGE with a mission to dive deeper into my offerings in my spa and to create my sales page for my "Day in the Life of An Ancient Greek Goddess Day" retreats.*

*I hired her as I was stuck on the correct language to use in my sales page and knowing we were of the same tribe, I knew Kris and I would speak the same language.*

*Our day together was playful, wise, insightful, deep, captivating, worldly and joyful. I didn't want it to end and in fact when my husband returned home from work that evening, he said I had a mischievous look on my face and that I was glowing. Yes I was! After a short time Kris emailed me some ideas and as soon as I read what she wrote, tears welled up in my eyes.*

*Kris captured my spirit and essence in one day of being together. I call her my Mystic sister."*

Being a part of Helen's world for a day made me realize how parched my own inner Aphrodite had been.

Take your pleasure and play, seriously. You'll soon see the benefits in all areas of your life, including your bank account.

# Pleasuring Yourself = Increasing Your Business

## Creativity + Productivity.

My intention for this chapter is to have you practice sacred sexuality and sensuality in ways that feel both safe and delicious for YOU.

**Part 1**. Make a list of activities to express your sensuality + sexuality that feel spine-tingly, fun and safe. For those of you feeling more adventurous and bold, GO FOR IT! Take off from wherever you are.

Here's my list (some of the items that are a bit more edgy *for me*—may be super tame for you—but I'm feeling the need to explore my boundaries):

- Using warm oil for self-massage
- Self-pleasuring with one of my many sex toys. Yep, sadly, they sit in a drawer most of the year
- Making love outdoors with my man
- Experimenting with tantric techniques for self-pleasuring and for sex with Shaun
- Practicing deep breathing
- Aromatherapy bathing with flower petals
- Dancing wildly alone
- Being naked
- Sleeping in a gorgeous silk nighty
- Slowly eating a delicious delight, like chocolate or coconut ice cream—no guilt allowed

**Part 2**. Choose at least one item on your list and engage in it BEFORE tackling your work. This is probably going to challenge you. I'm such a workaholic that I always use pleasure as a reward

AFTER my work is all done. And, quite often I forget to indulge in my reward.

But if you do something suweeet for yourself before even starting the work, my theory is that you'll be more energized, directed, creative and blissful when you approach your tasks.

We love flogging ourselves. So, let's just stop that once and for all... at least for today!

**Part 3.** Journal about your experience. Record how you felt about rewarding yourself with pleasure first.

- Were you more productive? More creative? Happier? Relaxed?

- Did it detract from your work in any way? What were your reservations/objections?

- If you found this to be a revelation, how will you include this in your work on a regular basis?

# Aphrodite's Role as Initiatrix

Even though she is the epitome and personification of Beauty, Pleasure, Delight, Sexuality and Sensuality, Aphrodite is not one to be trifled with. She is the Initiatrix, as we explored in her story the *Tale of Psyche + Eros.*

Aphrodite is also not one to overdo, overwork or over exert herself. She makes decrees and then spends her time being pampered by the ocean Nereids.

Let's just say she is the Mistress of Delegation.

How would it feel if you could make pronouncements and major decisions and then step back? Allow. Allow the Universe to meet your demands, rather than jumping on everything like a hungry lioness, controlling every outcome as if your life depended on it.

And really, who is in control ultimately?

One strategy that I find particularly Aphroditic is trusting that the Universe will hear your wishes and demands.

**I've seen the principle in my own business and life in two ways:**

1. I procrastinated on something to the point of feeling guilty and then everything turned out fine. In fact, if I had taken action sooner the results might have been disastrous.

2. I had an "I can't fucking take this one minute longer!" moment and just demanded that the Universe, my Ancestors, the Angels and Guides get it together so I could do the work I was put on earth to do! Then I landed the dreamiest client on the planet, who then referred 5 more of the dreamiest clients on the planet. That happened two weeks after I screamed and stamped my feet like a little 5 year old.

Oh yeah. Aphrodite acts that way sometimes too!

We are NOT gods or goddesses, but sometimes mythological figures themselves act like humans. They exhibit jealousy, anger, sadness, joy and every emotion in between.

**Brainstorm ways the strategy of trust + letting go has worked in your life and biz:**

1. Think of one or more examples when you let go and let the Universe take care of something you deeply needed or desired in the past (preferably a biz example, but if you can't come up with one use anything from your life). And it did a pretty fucking great job.

2. List one or more items you can give to the Universe for the next week or two and let it go. Keep track of synchronicities, chance meetings and resolutions that arise because of your receptivity.

3. Start each request for the Universe with "It would be nice if…" or "I'd love it if…"

Feel free to start with smaller or medium-sized requests and then work your way up from there.

Another way to look at giving the Universe some assignments is that you are lightening your load and taking some shit off of your "to do" list. And if there's a "real" person in your life you can delegate some stuff to, write their name and the task you will assign to them.

## Suggested Explorations

Use Psyche's tasks as a model to:

1. Sort out a huge pile of seeds: discernment. Separate priority projects from projects that can be delayed or cancelled.

2. Retrieve the Golden Fleece: empowerment. What is one thing that you fear but you know will help you in the long run? How can you face that fear with support, find allies

and know that even if you didn't feel like doing it, you 100% got it? Does perfection really matter? NO!

3. Fill a flask from the waterfall that flows from the River Styx: seeing the big picture. Are you continuing to play small, and not seeing how your brand fits into the larger world?

4. Return from the Underworld with a box of the beauty ointment of Persephone: learning self-discipline and soft focus. If you have to say no to some things and some people, what BIG looming task/s can you accomplish?

# Interview: Melissa Cassera

*Your brand and all of your offerings are all centered around "guilty pleasure." How did you come upon this as your unique brand archetype?*

I've always enjoyed guilty pleasures with wild abandon, including 3pm breaks to watch episodes of Gossip Girl (that sometimes turned into 3-hour marathons). I used to feel incredibly guilty indulging when I was supposed to be "working" until I realized: a) I'm the boss, and I make the rules, and b) I'm actually more productive when I take mandatory guilty pleasure breaks throughout the day. This led to my unique brand archetype, both because it was an authentic way I run my own business and because I knew it was something I could teach other people: *how to infuse more pleasure into your business.*

*Tell us about a few of your favorite characters and stories from childhood + how their essences have appeared in your work and brand.*

So, this might seem out of the norm of "childhood" but I grew up watching soap operas. *All My Children, Falcon Crest, General Hospital...* this was my everything. Cartoons? Not when Erica Kane was marrying her 14th husband.

I think I always knew from a young age that watching soap operas was salacious. I was hooked. I even penned soap-opera worthy stories about my 5th grade classmates, until I got in trouble for the gratuitous content (hey - I was a budding erotica writer, after all!).

Being hopelessly addicted to soap operas led to my current day brand. I became obsessed with "obsession." Why are people addicted to *Twilight,* or *Game of Thrones,* or Benedict Cumberbatch? And how can we model this in our businesses to create our own Obsessed audience?

*I adore that in your spare time you pen scandalous erotica novels and are working on a TV series about the supernatural. What's one (or two) pieces of advice you'd like to give to your entrepreneur fans that will help them create space for more passions and less promotion?*

1.  Remove distractions. This sounds easy but it's very difficult to be honest with yourself and admit you're spending too much time on Facebook or worrying about inconsequential things like how many Instagram likes your latest post received. I'm a fan of time blocking with no distractions. So, to get a work project completed, I will go to a coffee shop for a few hours and do it with no email, phone, social media, etc. That same task would normally take me days with distractions. Remove them, and you'll be amazed how much time you have left over to pursue your passions.

2.  Find a way to infuse your passions into your work. This is something I call the "Swirl Effect." If I'm completely lit up over erotic fiction, I'll make my latest blog post about how to get clients to behave like Christian Grey. Once I had to give a speech that I wasn't super excited about, until I changed the entire thing to talk about *Game of Thrones*. There's often a connecting thread between your work and your passions, which makes your life and work entirely pleasurable.

*From my own calculations of looking at other entrepreneur's timelines and after reading one of your blogposts ("Exposed! The inner workings of my business, revealed."), it takes about 10 years to get to a place where you're truly making bank and have thousands of adoring fans who will buy pretty much everything you create for them. Can you tell us a story about one turning point (I'm sure there are more) when you saw a real shift in your business? When you were thinking BIG and there was no resistance?*

Yes! Some people find success quicker than 10 years, even I was profitable with a fan base by year 2. It was just the wrong fan base and business model. I was pretending to be something I wasn't (buttoned-up, straight-laced business consultant) and I was attracting people that wanted that type of person. Recipe for disaster.

The biggest turning point was when I realized that revealing the parts of me that I tried to hide was GOOD for business. It happened in a conference room, with about 10 white-haired men, who were basically falling asleep during my presentation. Towards the end, one of the men asked me if he knew me. I shook my head "no," but he pressed on until he realized he had seen me in a local commercial. I was embarrassed, I always tried to hide that I was an actress because people wouldn't take me "seriously." I sunk into my chair and basically "gave up" on their business. But that moment, I was actually entirely ME. We chatted about the commercial, about my side career as a fledgling actress, and later that day I got the job and they were a client for many years.

Funny how the minute I wasn't pretending to be someone else was the minute I actually impressed them. It wasn't my PowerPoint slides, or my proposal, or my business suit. It was me - just being silly, goofy me.

### What is your *numero uno* favorite guilty pleasure?

Eeeek! That's hard. I gotta go with *Fifty Shades of Grey*. Or, *Gossip Girl*, Season 1. Or salted caramel, everything.

# Where Imagination Dwells

In the Introduction, I told you about the esoteric significance of the heart and its subtle energetic counterpart, the heart chakra.

This powerful spiritual center is often referred to as **The Rainbow Bridge** or **Astral Realm**. It is located at the center of the body and acts as the mediator between infinite potential (from the upper spiritual regions associated with the realm of Divine Intelligence and the world of ideas) and manifested reality (from the lower spiritual regions of feeling and the physical world).

As its title suggests, the Rainbow Bridge joins Being with Becoming; think of your imagination as a bridge where the many-colored Divine can meet your soul and become embodied in your everyday life and business.

It is the place where magic *happens*.

The term *astral* means "of the stars." We are literally made of stardust and the imagination can ignite the fire of inspiration that leads to the physical manifestation of our dreams. Without imagination our world is cold and gray, like a dead star.

Inner work, such as Imaginative Play (IP) and guided Vision Journeys (known as Pathworking), allows our consciousness to enter the Astral Realm; it's a similar state to the fluidity of your dreamtime during sleep. Images will appear and shift effortlessly.

The objective behind IP and Pathworking is to begin to shape the outer world to match the inner one.

# Meditation + Breathwork

**Focus:** Chakra 4, heart center Sanskrit: Anahata, Unstruck Sound

**Associations:** Love, center, balance, relationship, receiving, breath, submitting to higher will, and regal, romantic love. Feeling and embodiment.

**Planet:** Venus

**Day of the Week:** Friday

**Archetypes:** Shiva/Shakti union, Aphrodite, Tristan & Iseult, Kuan Yin, Jesus.

This chakra is located at the chest and unites the forces from the Cosmos with the forces of Earth. Inside the chakra is a hexagram, formed by upward and downward facing triangles that symbolize Shiva and Shakti in ecstatic union.

This is the seat of the imagination. What the eyes can't see and the brain can't wrap its head around, the heart knows to be true and real.

When we focus on this center, we sacrifice the ego to our Souls' higher plans.

Step 1: Begin to inhale slowly in a count of four through the petals of your heart chakra.

Step 2: Hold the breath for four counts, allowing the rich green light to expand and spread.

Step 3: When you exhale, breathe the green light out through the petals of your heart chakra into your aura, which surrounds your entire body.

Step 4: Hold your breath for four counts visualizing the green-colored light infusing your aura and bathing every cell of your body.

Repeat the pattern beginning with step 1 at least three more times.

To close the practice, breathe in Cosmic energy through your crown chakra and send the light down through your spinal column, then ground this energy deep into the heart of mother earth.

## Body Prayer

This simple body prayer movement sequence will help you feel sensual and free. Allow pleasure to spread through your entire body.

Put on your favorite music and spend 5-10 minutes doing an Aphrodite dance.

Pretend you are bathing in a secluded waterfall or grotto. The air is sweet with a fresh scent of water and blooming plumeria. Bend your knees and scoop up the water and then bathe yourself from head to toe. Breathe deeply and slowly. Any movement that is slow and sensual brings heightened awareness to your inner Aphrodite.

Look at yourself in the mirror afterwards. See how Aphrodite smiles back at you!

**Journaling Prompts:**

How does your work and life flow after doing your own sensual dance?

# Chapter 5: Shining Your Light

*"How would you behave if you were the best in the world at what you do?"*

**–Marie Forleo**

Marie's quote has inspired me to ask, if your Divine Self was CEO for a day how would you run your business?

And you can personify the form of your Divine Self however you like, i.e., Your Future Self, Aphrodite or Apollo or Rhiannon, etc. Approach your business through new eyes and see sparks of fun + magic!

Take your gifts and perform them as if you are the best in the world at what you do RIGHT NOW. As you are, no exceptions.

Here is where I find many entrepreneurs getting stuck:

*But I'm not ready to...*

*I don't know how to...*

*I need more time to...*

*I need more money to...*

The litany of objections goes on and on. This is why I elevate the imagination in this book. Without imagining a world where YOU are the best at what you do, it's not possible to make it a reality.

It takes courage to shine. You are being seen. Witnessed. Held. And this is both an empowering + vulnerable place to be.

As Tanya Geisler says all the time, "Your people want you to succeed."

For now, if you need, pretend you already have everything it takes to be the best in the world at what you do.

# Playing in the Field of Possibilities

**Part 1: What gift do you want to deliver right now?**

If you have more than one, list them.

**Part 2: Who do you need to be to deliver this gift?**

When you imagine yourself as the best in the world at this thing you do, be specific: what do you think about when you arise in the morning? What do you do? When problems materialize how do you solve them? What kind of marketing do you do to tell people about your gift?

**Part 3: Try this new you (of sweet greatness) out in your business for one day.**

Make this new you CEO for the day. Start by writing a manifesto or a simple memo. Write a blog post from this perspective. Make a new business plan for the year... the ideas are endless!

Be unreasonable. Imagine. Play.

# Case Study: Marie Forleo

*"Intuition rules. We trust our gut over everything else. We take big risks when it feels right and turn down revenue, opportunities and partnerships that, despite looking great on paper, give us that flash of intuitive doubt."*

**–Marie Forleo**

On the surface, entrepreneurial superstar Marie Forleo appears perfectly polished... until she starts clowning around on camera to hip hop music or has an emotional breakthrough on Oprah's Super Soul Sunday.

Forleo is a business force to be reckoned with, yet she is as approachable as your sweet next-door neighbor.

She became a best-selling author (*Make Every Man Want You: How to Be So Irresistible You'll Barely Keep from Dating Yourself!*) and created a multi-million dollar empire all before turning... 30.

Wowza.

**Marie's timeline:**

*2001: Quit publishing job, started coaching business.*

*2003: Kept coaching, but also became an MTV hip-hop choreographer/producer.*

*2005: Kept coaching, and also became one of the world's first Nike Elite Dance Athletes.*

*2006: Kept coaching, wrote and self-published book Make Every Man Want You.*

*2006-2008: Created 4 top-selling fitness DVDs.*

*2007 - 2008: Created first digital training programs, sold book to McGraw-Hill (now in 11 languages).*

*2009: Launched the first Rich Happy & Hot Mastermind, Virtual Coaching Program, and Live Event.*

*2010: Tony Robbins interview released; starting to experiment with video blogging, launched Rich Happy & Hot BSchool (online business education & mentoring program).*

*2011: Flew to South Africa with Richard Branson to work with Virgin Unite, partnered with Urban Zen for RHH Live, launched MarieTV.com.*

*(I think we can stop there.)*

*Holy shit. Master manifestor. Dynamo. Visionary.*

And she is also the first one to tell her legions of fans to just take action; begin no matter where you are at or how old you are.

She knows all things are possible. Not just because she believes, but because she has experienced it first hand:

> *"Everything is figureoutable. No matter what we want to create or make happen, we can figure it out. Google is the world's best free research assistant and social media allows us to connect with almost anyone on the planet to help bring our ideas to life, fast."*

The first time I saw **Marie TV** and witnessed her professionalism and finesse, I knew there was hope for me. And lots of other big dreamers.

It was one of those rare moments when I didn't feel a twinge of jealousy or comparison: I never said to myself, "Wow, this woman is rocking it like I never could." And truly surprised myself.

Okay, I'm not *greeeeen* with envy every time I meet someone successful, but look at that list of accomplishments again.

Wouldn't you think that would be crazy jealous-making?

And strangely enough, it isn't. It makes me sing the cosmic YES and has gotten me off of my ass when everything sucks.

Marie's particular form of magic galvanizes the entrepreneurial spirit. She transfers her positive and dynamic mindset to the people in her orbit. Even over the computer waves, while dispensing wise-for-her-years advice for entrepreneurs, she is capable of uplifting the consciousness of her viewers through the power of her own pure and light consciousness.

It may sound like a cross between science fiction and superstition, but it isn't.

Is she doing this consciously? Only she could tell us. According to one of the most famous 20th century occultists, Dion Fortune,

*"Magic is the art of causing changes to take place in consciousness in accordance with will."*

My archetypal analysis of Marie Forleo is that she is The Magician par excellence.

In myth and symbolism, the Magician is often pictured as Mercury, the messenger of the gods, holding his magic wand pointed upwards to the heavens. Mercury is swift, light, agile, intelligent and a master communicator in all media.

Being a best-selling author, sought-after speaker and pro vlogger Marie exemplifies all of these gifts.

The other implements surrounding the Magician are the sword, for discerning truth and cutting away that which is unnecessary; the pentacle (a disk with a five-pointed star of Venus in the center), for the power of earthly manifestation and attracting wealth; the cup, for the nourishment of divine love and enjoyment of sensual pleasures. Marie is the master of all of these elements.

And her gift of communication is also expressed as a Master Teacher. She opened **B-School** to rave reviews and fills the walls of her virtual academy with thousands of budding entrepreneurs each year. Without fail.

As of late, the Magician archetype is one that has captured the imagination of the masses.

Just think of Harry Potter or Merlin. Magic calls to us as a way to effectively move through the world. It is consciousness moved by the power of the will.

It's hard to imagine feeling magical while sitting in your corporate cubicle with no view of the outside world. With magic comes passion—and I can't think of a better way to live a magical, passionate life than to walk the entrepreneur's path.

Like the Magician who integrates all aspects of Self into a harmonious whole, entrepreneurship connects work and soul. To find meaning in our work is the greatest treasure we can hold. To make meaning be our work, that is poetry.

Marie Forleo shows us how it's done. And teaches us how to make our own magic.

***(Marie's case study first appeared on Rebelle Society.)***

# Myth of Amaterasu

One of the most powerful solar goddesses, Amaterasu, has dominated Japanese Shinto belief for centuries. (Other sun goddesses across the globe include Saule/Baltic, Sulis/Celtic Roman, Cybele/Mediterranean, and Sekhmet/Egyptian)

Her shrine was first built in Ise in the 7th century AD and is rebuilt every 21 years in the same spot, in exactly the same form.

Short version of her myth: She is born of the primordial couple and is so bright that they place her in the sky as the Sun.

Amaterasu's brother, the god of war, goes on a destructive rampage where he desecrates her quarters with his excrement.

As she looks down at the havoc, horrified, her brother pierces her with a spindle shaft. The metaphor of a spindle penetrating her represents the violation of rape.

Amaterasu retreats to a cave to hide out of shame, disgust and fear.

Her absence makes the world dark and cold, funereal. To woo her out of her cave, 800 deities decorate a tree with jewels, ribbons and mirrors and place it at the mouth of the cave, along with a large copper mirror fashioned by the smith goddess.

The shaman named no-Uzume, goddess of jollity, then performs a dance intended to restore the earth's fundamental energies. As the dance of the shaman grows more frenetic, she begins to undress and make jokes. In some myths she has the body of an old wrinkled woman who jiggles around her deflated breasts and stretches open her crinkly, ages old vagina!

The gods begin laughing so loudly that Amaterasu comes out of the cave to see what is going on. She catches her reflection in the copper mirror and is dazzled by her own radiance.

Amaterasu returns to the world, brings back the light and banishes her brother.

# Exploration: Shine On

Part of becoming a successful + fulfilled entrepreneur is challenging yourself to be a leader in your own realm. I know how difficult this can be. I'll share one of my personal stories about this.

In 2013, I created a paid membership group called the Enchanted Entrepreneurs Circle. I've always been the kind of leader who treads lightly. Unfortunately, I spent most of my time avoiding being a leader—I felt more comfortable in the role of collaborator.

This works to a point. But eventually, someone is going to step over a boundary or need real guidance.

The leader is the sovereign, remember that? Every sovereign has their own style; the leader's role is to define the vision of the group and to protect that vision.

In my group, I didn't post rules or guidelines. As a result, it sunk into a negative free-for-all, where everyone felt uncomfortable and no one knew who was "really" in charge.

At first, I felt angry as hell, "How dare these people not know who the leader is?"

My anger was a sign that something was out of integrity. And it was me. I was ignoring my role as vision holder; I got caught up in gossip and negative feelings.

After one month, my wonderful new group of 200 members was beginning to fall apart. I stepped in by strongly and lovingly laying out the guidelines for being in the group. The dissention completely evaporated. Problem members either came on board or left the group. There were no hard feelings. Just clarity. Anger is a call to see something more clearly.

My group is still going strong, two years later. The vision is being upheld by all with joy and enthusiasm because I stepped into the light as a leader AND a collaborator.

**The following journal prompts will help you bring aspects of yourself into the light that you may have been holding back.**

1. What is keeping you from shining like the sun? Is it fear? Feelings of uncertainty or doubt? Do you fear outshining others that you love and respect? (This is super common by the way.)

2. What are the healing roles of beauty and humor in your life? What can you do to cultivate them and bring you out of your dark moments?

3. Reflect on reflections: how seeing your beauty reflected back to you makes you want to shine more. Who can play the role of the magic mirror in your life? Who are those people you can count on to see your greatness, light and beauty… even in the midst of difficulties and darkness. Who will express and mirror your shine without resentment, jealousy or reservation?

# Interview: Tanja Gardner

I love diving into another entrepreneur's inner world. What I find there is the invisible essence that is being expressed visually and textually through their brand and marketing.

Tanja Gardner of **Conscious Introvert Success** and **Crystal Clarity Copywriting** has been a strengthening influence for me since we first met in 2012. It wasn't a huge surprise that she resonated most with a Scottish mythological figure named Scáthach. At first I was intrigued by the fact that Tanja regards herself as "deeply introverted." We often think introvert equals someone who is shy, a wallflower or consciously invisible. This is not the case with Tanja and many other introverts. In fact after I worked with Tanja, I came to realize I'm an introvert too!

Scáthach is a wise woman and a teacher of warriors (as well as their lover), who is known as the "The Shadow" and "warrior maid." I see Scáthach reflected in Tanja's indomitable spirit and excellence as a teacher and mentor.

***Your favorite figure from myth and story is Scáthach. What do you love most about her?***

Scáthach is definitely one of my favourite figures, and probably *the* most influential.

She's traditionally known as "The Shadowy One", although personally, I tend to refer to her as "Our Lady of the Boot to the Butt". She's a supernaturally powerful warrior (*some claim she's the daughter of the Morrigan herself*); but more than this, she's a trainer and teacher.

What do I love about her? Well, to start with, unlike many mythical female warriors who appear asexual, Scáthach gets laid. A *lot*. She's not a battle crone like her mother, or a shining virgin warrior like the Greek Athena.

In fact, one of Scáthach's stories describes her initiating the men she trained into both fighting arts and "the friendship of the thighs" equally. I assume she'd have shared a similar friendship with any female warriors she took under her wing too. That totally resonates with my own down-to-earth, pragmatic approach to sex.

On a less salacious note, I think what appeals to me most about her is her grounded, practical nature. She's not concerned with complex philosophical issues: she cares about getting the job done. She doesn't have a lot of patience for needless over complications either, which makes her a perfect counterpoint to my natural inner melodrama queen.

Finally, I love the fact that so much of her work is tied up in teaching and training others. While it's still hard for me to think of myself as a leader, I *have* always seen myself as a guide and mentor. So that's another aspect of her that I resonate strongly with.

### Did she choose you or did you choose her?

That's actually a hard question to answer. On the surface, I chose her: when I was training for ordination into the Fellowship of Isis, I had to identify the three goddess figures with whom I most identified. At the time, Scáthach was simply one of them.

And yet.

Since that moment of choosing, she's taken her place as the primary goddess in my psyche. And part of me suspects that, in as much as I believe in the objective existence of gods, I wouldn't have chosen her if she hadn't first chosen me.

### She has some kick-ass moves. She teaches martial arts—she's known for pole vaulting over fortress walls—and is skilled in underwater attack!

### As an entrepreneur what do you consider your killer moves to be?

Hmmmmmm… you know, I'd never seen myself as having "killer moves" until I answered this question!

Perhaps refusing to believe in "one right way" counts as a killer move? For me, that's about constantly trying to figure out what's right for me and forging my own path... and then taking a passionate stand for others to be able do the same for themselves. I see the people I work with as being the world's foremost experts in being *them*, and I refuse to act as though I know what's right for them better than they do.

Plus, maybe my talent for asking the right questions might count too. I've had clients in both my copywriting and my introvert work tell me how much clarity and insight they've gained from simply answering the in-depth questions I ask them. So knowing what to ask is probably one of my superpowers, and I'll happily claim it as a killer move here.

### How have her qualities of fierceness, sexuality and being a teacher/guide of heroes infiltrated your business?

Scáthach's is the energy that helps me live my "Fall down seven times, stand up eight" mantra whenever launches bomb and screw ups happen. That same energy also helps me remember my goals and motivates me to me get the practical, day-to-day stuff done to achieve them when all I want to do is slack off. (*Plus, it reminds me that I'm not superwoman, and that if I don't take care of myself and get enough rest and recharging, I won't be able to cope.*)

And of course, as an introvert coaching mentor, I take on the role of teacher and guide for other people. So connecting with that energy helps me to serve my clients as best I can.

### If you gave her an aspect of your biz to run, which would it be?

I'd start by asking Scáthach to manage my daily task list! Gods know I need help keeping it to sane levels, and prioritising it sensibly. I'd tell her my end goals, and what was most important to me. Then I'd rely on her to filter through my eleventy billion task reminders and tell me what I *really* needed to do each day.

After that, I might put her in charge of purchasing/resourcing decisions too. I regularly suffer from Shiny Object Syndrome for both business training programmes and tools/resources. I always want to sign up for ALL THE THINGS; and I then wonder why I keep getting overwhelmed.

So I'd give her the power of veto over every single training- or resource-related decision I make. If something didn't support my long-term goals (*or would just overwhelm me*), I'd rely on her to be the giant "NO!" voice I needed to hear.

### What business advice does Scáthach want to share with entrepreneurs?

Two (*possibly contradictory*) pieces of advice come to mind when I ask this question within:

- **You can ask for the help you need**: Scáthach's a trainer and guide who helps people become better and more skilled than they ever could on their own. Likewise, in your business there are people who want to teach you, guide you and support you just waiting to connect with you—but you usually need to reach out to them before they can help.

- **You don't have to accept anyone else's way of doing anything in your business**: different martial arts styles suit different people, and no one practice fits everyone. In the same way, there's no one right way to run your business: you need to figure out what works for you, and make the final decision on whether something's right for you or not.

# Meditation + Breathwork

**Focus**: Chakra 3, Solar Plexus

**Sanskrit**: Manipura, lustrous gem

**Associations**: Fire, Power, Vitality, Energy, Movement, Lion, Ram, Will, Autonomy, Drive and Transformation

**Planet**: Mars, Sun

**Day of the Week**: Tuesday

**Archetypes**: Magician, Warrior, Apollo, Lugh, Ares/Mars, Sekhmet, Chango, Mawu, Amaterasu

Step 1: Begin to inhale slowly in a count of four through the petals of your solar plexus chakra.

Step 2: Hold the breath for four counts, allowing the golden-yellow warmth to expand and spread, as if you're running sunshine throughout your body.

Step 3: When you exhale, breathe the gold light out through the petals of your solar plexus chakra into your aura, which surrounds your entire body.

Step 4: Hold your breath for four counts visualizing the yellow-gold light infusing your aura and bathing every cell of your body.

Repeat the pattern beginning with step 1 at least three more times.

To close the practice, breathe in Cosmic energy through your crown chakra and send the light down through your spinal column, then ground this energy deep into the heart of mother earth.

## Body Prayer

This easy body prayer movement sequence will increase courage and radiance. It's basically the yoga stance known as Warrior's Pose.

This can be done indoors or out. Stand with your legs wide apart. Move your right foot so it faces to the right and begin bending your right leg slightly.

Raise both arms out to the sides, up to your shoulders and turn your head and face to the right.

Take a deep breath and as you are gazing into the horizon image your future self standing in front of you. This you is radiant, fulfilled, healthy, affluent and joyful. See how they hold their body, how they're dressed, the style of their hair and make up.

This self is doing this same stance facing you and eventually your outstretched hands come closer together, your fingers touching.

Feel your future self's positive and enlivening energy flowing into you and spreading throughout your body, infusing every cell with more radiance and confidence.

### Journaling Prompts:

Journal about your experience and remember how you felt—bring the memory into your body any time you feel fear or are breaking through your own glass ceiling and need an extra dose of courage.

# Chapter 6: Engaging the Trickster

*"Let me tell you that when a woman starts out to be tricky, she can beat a man every time, because her mind works a heap faster and she sees all around and over and underneath and on both sides of a thing while he's trying to stare plumb through it."*

**–Kathleen Ragan,** *Fearless Girls, Wise Women and Beloved Sisters*

**Nothing in our world would change or transform without the creative + disruptive energy of Trickster.**

As you'll find in the pages to follow, I'm obsessed with the Trickster archetype. In my dissertation I worked with the Female Trickster as one of the archetypes informing the work of female drummers in Brazil and around the world.

Many Trickster aspects are applicable to our work in branding and marketing:

- **Visibility + Invisibility**. Trickster reveals as it conceals. Fears of being visible and invisible are the most common roadblocks for the hundreds of entrepreneurs I've come in contact with. Hermes, the Greek messenger god, exemplifies the powers of invisibility; he appears exactly at the right time and then slips away. Harry Potter, with his invisibility cloak steps into Trickster territory in more than one installment of JK Rowling's series.

- **Fluidity + Transformation**. Trickster can cross any boundaries and move easily between the worlds because it's a liminal being. Shadow figures and Shape Shifters that we encounter in stories and our lives often belong to this archetype. Bo from *Lost Girl*, as well as many other characters in that show, are boundary crossers and shape shifters.

- **Innovation**. There are numerous examples of hero and heroine Tricksters in myth, film, TV and literature. Heroes often trick or outsmart the status quo to bring in a new world order. In Greek mythology, Prometheus stole fire from the gods to help humanity.

Trickster is a great awakener—sometimes through humor, pure shock value or subversiveness. At other times Trickster can simply ask, "What if…" and turn the world upside down.

Not surprisingly, many Trickster figures such as Hermes/Mercury act as messengers of the Gods and intermediaries between deities and humans. Tricksters can be both angelic and demonic. They are masters of the marketplace and are invoked at the crossroads for protection and good fortune.

Be wary. As fun, engaging and innovative as these Tricksters are, their very nature is to sneak up on you when you aren't paying attention. They are the cracks and holes that important details can slip through. Ooops!

(Just think of Mercury Retrograde times!)

And… without those cracks there would be no opening for the new.

Like Wile E. Coyote, Trickster is prone to self-delusion; there are few easier to fool than the Fool himself/herself.

Have the faith of the Fool; leap into the void regularly. Nothing is more exhilarating than being the Fool for a time and allowing the Cosmos to carry you to the other side. You will end up somewhere unexpected, that's for sure.

# Time to Break Up with "Normal" Marketing

Tricksters we have come to know and love share common characteristics: their capacity to create new life, their ability to shapeshift, their connection with the realm of the dead, and particularly, their facility to upset the balance of power in order to bring equilibrium to their mythological universes. For the Trickster there is no question of asking for permission or doubting that they have the right to have or do what they wish.

Trickster is both ancient and postmodern. Like the Female Trickster Molly Cotton-Tail introduced in the epigraph of this chapter, Female Trickster figures are not bumbling or unconscious like their predominantly male counterparts. Female Trickster figures see many paths, skillfully navigate them, and steal supernatural skills from the strong male compatriots in their mythologies.

Tricksters are full of contradictions and have qualities that make them more human-like than other supernatural beings. They move and shape-shift in their divine state of being; however, they also experience human feelings and emotions.

The Trickster is not concerned with preserving tradition, favoring instead to breathe new life into old outmoded forms.

Ricki Tannen, author of *The Female Trickster: The Mask That Reveals, Post-Jungian and Postmodern Psychological Perspectives on Women in Contemporary Culture*, views humor as an important aspect of the Female Trickster archetype. She points out that "humor and irony with movement results in a boundary-crossing process-oriented, postmodern Trickster" (176).

Trickster, especially the female variety, often uses humor to reclaim its power.

# Female Tricksters :: Models of Transformation + Dynamism

The Brazilian-West African goddess Oya-Iansá, a dynamic figure and powerful agent of change, transcends her roles as mother and queen. However most scholars would not consider her a part of the Trickster archetypal family. The act of re-imagining her as Female Trickster transforms her relationship within the orixá (the gods in African mythologies) and human spheres.

As a Trickster, Iansá is functionally capable of dissolving boundaries and rules in order to recreate the balance of power in her world. Re-ordering the world is Trickster archetypal energy in action.

One way this is accomplished is through the imagination. The power of imagination is highly valued in the worldview of a Trickster, and this trait marks why it is so important to business, technology and marketing.

Corporate bodies cling tightly to their hierarchies and rules, even when these are no longer beneficial.

Without the Trickster figure to question the existing structures, there will not be room for creativity and innovation, and progress will cease. The Trickster figure imagines a new reality and then finds a way to bring it into being, often through deception because the old order will not give in without a fight.

One story that illustrates Iansá's Female Trickster aspect is the tale of her theft of the power to create lightning and fire from her second husband Xangô (pronounced "Shango").

The film *Orixás da Bahia* produced by Lázaro Faria, highlights Iansá's transgression and ingenuity in an animated version of the myth:

At the beginning of time Xangô sent Iansã, mistress of winds and storms, his most important wife, to bring him a potion that would let him breathe fire from his nose and mouth.

Iansã disobeyed him and tasted the potion on her way back, so that she could breathe fire too.

This made Xangô furious because he had wanted to keep that power all to himself. Without Iansã, Xangô cannot make fire.

Xangô is inseparable from Iansã.

(Orixás 13:50-14:28)

In a different version of the story, Iansã steals the secret of fire from Xangô after he begins an affair with another female orixá, Oxum. Even though their marriage was not exclusive (Xangô is married to two other orixás) Iansã becomes Xangô's primary female counterpart because without her he cannot produce lightning or fire.

Iansã is jealous of Xangô's affair with Oxum, so she spies on them and gets upset.

Instead of wallowing in self-pity or even turning against Oxum, Iansã steals Xangô's secret to creating lightning so he can never be parted from her. Iansã's actions demonstrate how the Female Trickster is set apart from the jilted wife:

> "[…] to move psychologically beyond identification as a victim to identification as your own unique self utilizing your wit as the process which transforms pathos into pleasure is postmodern Trickster" (Tannen 179).

Like all classic Tricksters, Iansã crosses many boundaries. She is a psychopomp (one who carries souls over the threshold of death to the Otherworld), the bringer of storms, destroyer of anything old and outworn, the patroness of independent and outspoken women and the ruler of the marketplace.

Trickster represents the *"what if"* energy of all possibilities, seen and unseen, which can break through at any time. Campbell describes the trickster figure as one who opens up paths that were once forbidden or unheard of. "The mind structures a lifestyle, and the ool or trickster represents another whole range of possibilities. He doesn't respect the values that you've set up for yourself, and smashes them" (An Open Life 39).

# Case Study: Halley Gray

*"So much has been done, exclaimed the soul of Frankenstein—more, far more, will I achieve; treading in the steps already marked, I will pioneer a new way, explore unknown powers, and unfold to the world the deepest mysteries of creation."*

### –Victor Frankenstein

*Frankenstein*; or, *The Modern Prometheus*, written by Mary Shelley is hailed as one of the first works of science fiction and filled with all of the sturm und drang of Victorian Romanticism.

I see parallels of this 1818 novel to the passion-filled rhetoric of modern solopreneurs.

Without passion and enthusiasm it is not possible to pave our unique path in this over-saturated world of marketing and media.

It takes tremendous courage and chutzpah to be yourself and "pioneer a new way."

Halley Gray of Evolve + Succeed has her own storm brewing and is creating quite a stir in the online marketing realm as the strategist who can get entrepreneurs booked out for months at a time.

**Truth**

- Michelle Ward, When I Grow Up Coach, worked with Halley in 2012 and as a result was booked out eight months in advance.

- Angie Mroczka, author + publisher, worked with Halley and tripled her income.

- Kat McBride, visual artist, went from $0 to $4,000 revenue.

- Sas Petherick is booked out months in advance for her coaching practice.

I've known Halley since 2012 and have always loved her independent spirit and deep desire to help other entrepreneurs.

And the fact that she swears, dons fun turquoise eyeglasses, creates new marketing terms like "salesnado" and compares the ubiquitous big red "buy now" buttons to Patch Adams' nose… makes me truly and madly love this woman.

The archetypes that Halley is articulating and amplifying through her brand are Mad Scientist and Trickster Heroine.

She recently professed to me that her favorite characters and real people include Indiana Jones, Lawrence of Arabia, Dr. Victor Frankenstein (she adores the Mel Brooks film version, Young Frankenstein), and a ground-breaking female marine biologist who studied sharks, pirates and ship captains.

Halley's fascination with Dr. Frankenstein developed because instead of following the universal laws of nature, he goes ahead and does what everyone says can't be done. She adores science and is inspired by those who find ways to go beyond the limits of convention and the tried and true.

Her love of Anti-Heroes such as Indiana Jones points to her courageous and adventurous Trickster Heroine connection.

The Greek hero Prometheus, who created humans out of clay, and then later disobeys the gods and gives fire to humankind, suffers the penalty for breaking the divine laws: each day Prometheus is chained to a boulder while an eagle devours his liver.

Eew.

Symbolically, the liver was the seat of the emotions to the Greeks and Prometheus' eternal punishment was to be internally dismembered. The next morning, though, his liver would heal and be completely restored.

Typically solopreneurs often feel like lone, cray-cray, innovative, mad scientists as they pave the way for all the other entrepreneurs coming up behind them. The Prometheus myth clues us into the fact that breaking new ground is dis-membering just as it is re-membering.

To create something new we have to first destroy the world and then put it back together again. The Trickster, possibly more than any other archetype, has the ability to heal the splits we suffer so often in post-modern life.

Like Dr. Frankenstein who turns death into life, Halley resuscitates the dead heart of a business so it can beat again.

# The Liminal: Trickster Archetypal Energy

Tricksters function outside the rules of society; they resist boundaries and categories. Most Trickster figures rule over liminal, transitional places, like an entrance, doorway, or threshold, places where anything can happen. In society, people who live on the margins can also be termed "liminal." As Turner explains, "Liminal entities are neither here nor there; they are betwixt and between the positions assigned and arrayed by law, custom, convention, and ceremonial" (The Ritual 95).

To Marion Woodman, Jungian therapist and author, individuation is a process that bridges the split between the feminine and the masculine aspects of psyche. Woodman emphasizes that women and men embody the feminine and masculine archetypes differently.

For a woman, the individuation process puts her in a state of vulnerability within herself as a feminine being, completely whole within herself "confident enough to be consciously vulnerable" (Woodman, Pregnant Virgin 85) and who "can make her own choices; she can be who she is because that is who she is" (Woodman, Addiction to 182). The Female Trickster's actions mirror her inner authority.

Woodman points out that successful career women, who are often accepted by society and their male peers, are not necessarily models of integrated, fulfilled people: "If we look at the modern Athenas sprung from their father's foreheads, we do not necessarily see liberated women. Many of them have proven beyond question that they are equal to or better than men [...]. But they are also, in many cases, unhappy women" (Woodman, Addiction to 9). I would argue that they are not Female Tricksters either. In becoming powerful in their careers, some women did not determine success on their own terms; instead they fit themselves into the male-centric model provided to them.

Taking on the man's world and a man's concerns is different from expressing feminine assertiveness. The distinction is subtle, in that strong feminine energy supports a woman to grow and expand in the way she desires, regardless of what a society considers normal and acceptable for her station in life.

Creative and innovative men have also suffered a similar fate in the hands of corporations. They are regarded as successful as long as they follow THE rules. They stuff their feelings and opinions in order to fit in and stay on track for a promotion. After sacrificing their family's happiness and their own need for intimacy, these men become empty husks; their souls have been pulled into the depths of the underworld, which often creates addictions to sex, drugs, alcohol and power.

Trickster is the most sexually ambiguous of the archetypes. Another sign of its need to not conform to "normality" and social conventions. We all need to break free of society's oppressive rules from time to time. Humor, sex and breaking traditions + taboos are all ways the Trickster overtakes us.

# Suggested Explorations in the Realm of Trickster

Is your marketing like everyone else's? What can you change in your branding that will stamp it with your unique essence?

List out the marketing and branding initiatives you have taken during the past year.

Place a star next to the ones that brought you the most fulfillment… you can include the highest number of sign ups, most money, most fun to do and most engaging for your customers as markers of "fulfillment."

What can you create to shake up the old routines in your marketing and branding?

As much as we are told that our audiences love consistency and predictability, I've found that I get a huge kick out of surprising my tribe. And the results are always superlative because they respond so positively!

Wake up your subscribers with a fresh new newsletter, video or blogpost.

# Interview: Karey Pohn

*Entrepreneurs are liminal beings, i.e., many don't have set schedules and are rule breakers. What other qualities do you think make entrepreneurs more "Tricksterish" than other more corporate-minded folks?*

Entrepreneurs are very much like Tricksters, they are always breaking new ground, creating things that have never been done before, or giving a new twist to something old that brings it alive and current. They are culture creators—think Steve Jobs or Walt Disney. They combine and recombine things in new and creative ways, like Hermes. Tricksters are culture bringers, and entrepreneurs bring new things to culture. They think outside the box and "boldly go where no man has gone before," to quote a line from *Star Trek*.

Entrepreneurs, like Tricksters, are adventurous, like to try new things, and like to upset the established order just for the fun of it. They often don't fit in. Both the entrepreneur and the Trickster see things in a different way. They help us to see and do things differently too. They often see opportunities others might miss.

They like to play around, and "tinker" with things. Sometimes entrepreneurs can be found inside larger organizations, but typically they are found on the edges, at the frontiers, like Doug Engelbart, the guy who invented the mouse. Doug wanted to help people to think better.

Because the Trickster element is so strong in entrepreneurs, they need to watch out for the fact that Tricksters often get tricked in the process—just think of Wile E. Coyote. He is a prime example of a Trickster who gets tricked and badly!!! The joke is often on them, which can be very costly, in many ways.

*You talk about the game of life and the concept of play rather than "getting played"... can you say something about that?*

*How can entrepreneurs participate in "The Game" and come out with confidence and peace of mind, even if they get played?*

My friend, astrologer and coach Laurence Hillman has a saying: *"you do the gods, or the gods do you."* What he means by this is that one has to consciously honor the gods—the archetypal principle that the gods personify—or you will unconsciously be at the effect of that principle. My doctoral work was on the archetypal aspects of play—how we can see life as a "cosmic game" which we can play consciously through understanding archetypal principles, or be played by these energies, and end up feeling like a shuttlecock in badminton, being volleyed back and forth or a ball on a squash court getting slammed into various walls all the time. We need to play the game, be the player, or we will indeed be played, like the shuttlecock or the squash ball!

When we understand different archetypes, it allows us get our archetypal bearings, and with each archetype comes a set of qualities or properties. When you enter the territory of a specific archetype, it's like being in another country, where they have different ways of doing things, customs, protocols, etc. It is useful to know what kind of things you can expect when you visit a different country, the weather, the different places you can go and things you can do. It allows you to have more fun and to make sense of things. If you arrive in a place and have no idea where you are or what's going on, it can be quite disorienting and scary. You might miss out on some amazing experiences.

I like to use different maps and models to orient myself. If you have a map or guidebook, you'll have a better time. It's the same with the concept of archetypes—if we know the different archetypes, we can be on the lookout for places where we can use their unique gifts, or beware of the potential pitfalls they can create.

We can play with them, and go with the flow instead of swimming upstream. Our brains like certainty and maps help us to make sense of our experiences and to know what to expect. When we don't have this, we can't think as clearly. Our limbic systems can run the show and we can easily end up in fight or flight. When our brains aren't happy, no one is happy.

For example, with Tricksters, we know that they are chaotic and like to break the rules, yet they often get tricked by their own tricks. As an entrepreneur, we want to be on the lookout for how we might be tricking ourselves, might we be too outside the box, so that no one wants what we have to offer? Or are we being outrageous at the wrong times. How might we package our creations or ourselves in a way that people who might be more traditional might accept them, if that is what we need. If we have an idea that is important, and we need to get a bank loan, do we really need to get that new nose ring before we go to meet with the loan officer in Dubuque, Iowa—San Francisco, perhaps, but lets not get too out there.

Is our chaotic nature getting in the way? Do we not have enough structures in place or have too many plates spinning or files open in the hard drives of our mind—and do we crash and burn because of this? Do we need to hire an accountant or an assistant to make sure vital areas of our lives are being tended to. These are ways that we can use archetypal knowledge to troubleshoot not only situations, but our own psychological tendencies, and then find ways to support ourselves both in our businesses and our lives.

Back to the Tricksterish nature of entrepreneurs, and getting played. If we know that we have a tendency towards chaos, and that this is not optimal for the brain, we can possibly adapt our behaviors so that we don't tip over the edge. We need to be able to surf that wave, not get buried by it. One great thing to do is to avoid multitasking and to focus on one thing at a time and minimize distractions.

David Rock wrote a great book that I think that all entrepreneurs can benefit from. It's called *Your Brain At Work*. It is written using stories, and gives lots of good information about how you can work with your brain instead of against it. I was so impressed by it that I actually became a brain-based coach with his Neuroleadership Group.

Tricksters and entrepreneurs are also prolific players, they are able to engage in make believe—and ask "what if" questions, imagining things that don't exist yet. They are often able to create their own realities. This "what if" thinking can be used in a good way to anticipate obstacles, and then think up creative solutions, but it can turn against us when we catastrophize. Building mountains out of molehills is not a really great way to be creative, unless you are creating a game that will go viral, like Angry Birds.

***Can you describe some good examples of how one of your favorite characters would solve your biggest business conundrums?***

Mary Poppins, my all-time favorite character, and my role model perfectly personifies wonderful ways of solving problems. First of all, her signature song—"Spoonful of Sugar" helps us to find the fun in things that we do, thus keeping our brains in a happy state. I use this to trick myself into doing things that I don't like to do that are essential, like accounting. To paraphrase Mary, if I can find the fun in every job that must be done—"snap, the job's a game, and every task you undertake becomes a piece of cake."

Mary is an example of a Trickstar, someone who tricks people for their own good or the greater good. An example of this is to gamify things. It's all the rage these days and that's because as a species, we are indeed *homo ludens*, man the player—we stay young as a species our entire lives. We are the only species that retains childlike characteristics into adulthood—our nearest relatives, chimpanzees look like old people when they are quite young, whereas we essentially look like young chimps our whole lives. You can go a long way with play and gamification.

Mary also is great at reframing situations, and getting into her customer's [the Banks family] model of the world, and seeing what they need and delivering it in a way that works. Perhaps not in the way they would imagine it, but in a way that helps everyone in the end. She has the long view in mind and knows that sometimes old ways of being need to die before new ones are born.

But she also sees to it that support is provided in the chaotic times in between.

Mary sees that the children need structure and she playfully provides this, helping them to learn lessons through imaginative play, and outings of every sort. She helps George Banks to break out of the rut of routine that has his whole family in a ghastly mess.

And she has fun the entire time, and so do most of the others. Speaking of the rut of routine and getting stuck—*The War of Art* by Steven Pressfield is the best book ever about this. A total must read for anyone involved in any creative or meaningful endeavor. Now back to Mary—she finds ways of getting her message across in ways that others will understand and resonate with. She is able to help others to see things her way through great rapport and caring, knowing when to pace and when to lead.

Mary also helps people see things they might have missed, like the Bird woman, and to focus on what is really important—being kind and generous with our time and ourselves instead of unconsciously remaining in old outworn habits, hoarding and being cross.

People and consciousness are our most important assets, and Mary helps people to change and transform and helps others to see things differently, do things differently, to learn and evolve, and have fun in the process! This is the most important thing—because it helps the brain to get behind the change, which can be a scary thing for the brain. When we are able to play, hold things loosely, imagine different ways of doing things and share our dreams with others in ways that they will find enticing, like Mary, things go better. We think better and we are better.

We can bring out the best in others when we know more about the brain, Mary and Disney intuitively knew this. Through the latest cutting edge research on neuroscience, by reading people like Lou Cozolino, Daniel Siegel and Matt Lieberman, just like Mary, we can remain in the lovely liminal land between the two banks of chaos and rigidity, in the sweet space of possibility!!!

# Meditation + Breathwork

**Focus**: Chakra 2, Sacral (located just below the belly button)

**Sanskrit**: Svadhisthana, sweetness

**Associations**: Water, Ocean and Other Bodies of Water, Emotions, Pleasure, Sexuality, Desire, Change, Trickster, Shapeshifters, Movement, Intimacy and Creativity

**Planet**: Jupiter

**Day of the Week**: Thursday

**Archetypes**: Prometheus, Hermes, Loki, Eros, Coyote, Oya, Oshun, Mami Wata, Changing Woman, Proteus, Werewolves and Mermaids

We are all creators in our lives and this spiritual center, associated with the center called Yesod on the Tree of Life in Kabbalah, is likened to the "engine room" of creation.

When we create intentionally, **we make magic**, pure and simple.

This center is connected to the Ethereal realm which is also where my mer guides have contacted me from. Morgen, who told me she was a conglomeration of nine spirit sisters, said that the mer enter into us through the ethereal realm and swim up to our heart centers. In essence, they were bringing the intense energy from the base and sacral chakras up to our heart centers where we can fertilize our love + imagination with our creativity.

Step 1: Begin to inhale slowly in a count of four through the petals of your pelvic chakra.

Step 2: Hold the breath for four counts, allowing the orange-colored energy to expand and spread.

Step 3: When you exhale, breathe the orange light out through the petals of your pelvic chakra into your aura, which surrounds your entire body.

Step 4: Hold your breath for four counts visualizing the orange light infusing your aura and bathing every cell of your body.

Repeat the pattern beginning with Step 1 at least three more times.

To close the practice, breathe in Cosmic energy through your crown chakra and send the light down through your spinal column, then ground this energy deep into the heart of mother earth.

## Body Prayer

Move your body to something rhythmic and elemental, like **Gabrielle Roth and the Mirrors, 5 Rhythms percussion music**. Emphasize snake-like movements in your arms and hands. Spiral the hips. Pretend you are Fire itself, feeling the consuming aspect of yourself. Then switch to Water. Flow—move into the gaps, go deep.

Be the Fool and dance like no one is watching.

**Journaling Prompts:**

How do you "feel" into your elemental places?

How easily can you move between two elements? Is is a quick adjustment or does it take time?

# Chapter 7: The Spiral Journey Home

*"The privilege of a lifetime is being who you are."*

**–Joseph Campbell**

We've made it to the home zone and we end at the beginning.

The idea to use a story as a brand map came to me while in a state of reverie. Our business reflects our soul's purpose in action in the world.

My theory is that the map of your brand will mirror the map of your soul.

Later in this chapter, I will use *The Alchemist* to show how to fuse your favorite story into your brand mapping process. I chose *The Alchemist* because it transcends cultural boundaries; it's likened to a myth, legend or a fairy tale because it applies to everyone, everywhere, at any time. It's magical like that!

Through storytelling you take your audience on a journey, rather than just giving them a superficial overview of their marketing needs. Data has its place, of course. People come to us as experts because they're looking for help, solutions and answers to their questions. Yes, it's our duty to provide tangible help. But we can't stop there.

A *soulful* brand map gives you a deeper understanding of the imaginal, emotional and psychological places your soul has traveled. It points to who you are becoming and where you're headed. And, it helps you reorient your clients to their own soul maps.

Archetypal psychology and mythology connect us to our soul's purpose and reanimates the world with shimmering magical splendor. As above, so below. As it is inside us, so it is in the outside world.

It doesn't take a brain surgeon to see that re-imagining your business to reflect your own archetypal tendencies feels magical and exciting!

Archetypes reinforce what we know to be true of ourselves and our greatest gifts. Myths and stories map out how our primary archetypal energies work in relation to the world and the Other.

When we share our stories we heal. We transform. We touch each other's hearts and minds.

Let's use storytelling rather than just data-dumping when we promote, market and brand our businesses. The world will be a better place and we'll probably sell more too.

# Case Study: Amethyst Mahoney

Amethyst's story is heroic and takes many twists and turns. Her favorite book, *The Odyssey*, follows the prototypical Hero's Journey that we see in thousands of films and books throughout history, up to the present. These plots and patterns show up in animated Disney films and in science fiction blockbusters, such as Star Wars. Harry Potter's classic Hero's Journey made J.K Rowling the millionaire she is today. The variety of tales are endless, but the archetypal journey is the same.

Why do we never tire of such stories? I re-read *The Alchemist* nearly every year. Stories about heroes and heroines evoke inspire us to rise above our limitations and see our dreams all the way through. Like the hero we deal with setbacks, disappointments, defeat. We meet mentors, allies, enemies (the Shadow) and lovers who betray us (the Shapeshifter).

As a collective, we relate to the hero more than any of the other archetypes.

A little backstory on our heroine: Amethyst grew up in Memphis, Tennessee. Her family was so poor that they moved every eight or nine months—the time it took for the bill collectors to locate them.

Raised Southern Baptist, Amethyst's whole childhood was about control. One day, when she was 12 years old, she was selling Girl Scout cookies, candy for school, and other goodies. When she handed over $300 to her teacher she thought to herself, "*I haven't eaten in 2 days. If I sold things for MYSELF, I could keep some of this money.*"

That summer Amethyst formed a partnership with a friend and went door to door selling "Googly Eyed Critters." She got to eat and an entrepreneur was born!

Now she has clients in more than 175 countries around the world.

But in true heroic fashion, she decided that wasn't enough. She wanted clients in her own neighborhood so she began *Googling* and contacting local business owners.

The hero always brings the *boon*, the reward for her trials and tribulations, back to the village.

Amethyst's success did not just happen because of her ability to rise above her humble beginnings, nor was it just because she overcame fear and took action. It happened because she is a talented and skilled community builder.

Her Spiritual Badass Facebook group has changed names and logos multiple times, but her consistency in mixing nurturing support with humorous and fun diversions keeps her tribe hooked. (Yep, that includes me.)

*"There are almost no networking communities specifically designed for healers and coaches. Most focus on brick-and-mortar type businesses, and they do NOT get us. Everyone I talk to about this is crazy excited! I realized when I started talking about it, I was no longer afraid. I did not worry about what others would think, or if I was good enough. I realized that I really have stepped up and started standing as a beacon of light for those who think there is no one else out there like them. And instead of wanting to hide, I only wanted to shine brighter."*

Amethyst's tip for everlasting business bliss: Talk to people!

Every day find one person to ask, "How can I help you?" You'll be amazed at what opportunities will come up!

*"Stop waiting for permission from your Guides, or yourself, or your mommy or daddy. You are already good enough. Just start offering to help because it's really not about you anyway... And for God's sake, stop sweating over a business card and what to call yourself. Nobody really cares about that. They just want to know how you can help them."*

And, one other thing that I absolutely love about Amethyst is her purple hair... her pink bob... and also her silver sparkly tresses.

The woman changes her hair, her brand and her mind whenever she damn pleases. I call that sovereignty and extreme authenticity!

She is one to keep watching. Believe me, you'll never get bored.

# *The Alchemist* by Paulo Coelho as a Brand Map

For the final leg of this journey I chose to highlight the themes prevalent in Paulo Coelho's *The Alchemist*. Not only do I re-read it every other year or two, but I've bought it for countless other people because it is an amazing map into the anatomy of dreams.

You don't need to read or re-read the book now, however it will help you invoke the mystery of how the universe directs the course of our lives and businesses.

The best way to work with the brand mapping material is to work on it in small chunks, in thirty-minute to one-hour sprints, over two to three weeks. If you prefer to do the whole thing in one day, go for it. But then put it away for five to seven days, let it marinate and then come back to refine your work.

## Dreaming the Landscape of Your Business

> *"It's the possibility of having a dream come true that makes life interesting, he thought..."* (*The Alchemist*, p. 11)

> *"Dreams are the language of God."* (p. 12)

Santiago is a dreamer, but he questions the size of his dream and wonders what else is out there for him. One of his dreams is to marry the daughter of the baker in town. But he wonders if having a shepherd for a husband can be "enough"?

How often do you feel not enough? Supernaturally creative entrepreneurs, like you and me, are too often haunted by *not enoughness.*

Our internal voices rage:

*You're not selling enough.*

*You're not doing enough.*

*YOU are not enough.*

**This voice blinds the TRUTH.**

The truth is that you were born ENOUGH. Whole. Complete. You were designed perfectly imperfect.

You have a Personal Legend. Something that enraptures + embodies your spirit. A story that needs to radiate through the universe.

Realizing your Personal Legend is all you need to start living a life and business filled with power, imagination and ease. Because taking action, even small baby steps, depends on listening to your heart's messages.

*And...* it doesn't usually happen overnight. The important part about seeking your Personal Legend is to go deep and sense with your intuition where you are being led.

Find your hidden treasure.

For each of us "the" dream, or as Coelho puts it, your Personal Legend, is unique. We are born knowing what it is. It is our conditioning—the cultural and family dramas—that pulls us away from that center. In our quest to individuate ourselves, often through our livelihoods, we go on adventures, take many wrong turns, fall in love, fall apart and lose ourselves.

Yet, by some miracle we always end up exactly where we need to be. It is my mission to help other entrepreneurs learn to trust in the invisible, and even invite it for tea.

Set a timer for ten minutes:

- What is the role of dreams in your business?
- What do you wish for with all of your heart?

- How have your wishes + dreams changed over the past year? Have they grown/expanded? Or have they become simplified?

**Dreams are powerful omens and recycling tools.** You can see images that point to where you are heading and re-live the feelings you had during current or past experiences.

As a child I had hundreds of flying dreams, and now I have flying daydreams! I incorporate the theme of triumph and freedom in my brand (like my winged Melusine woman logo), since these are clearly important to me.

Santiago has a recurring dream about a child who plays with his sheep and who then advises him to go to the Egyptian Pyramids to find his treasure.

At the moment the child is about to point out the exact location, Santiago wakes up.

Set your timer for fifteen minutes:

- Can you think of one or more dreams you've had in your life that reflects where you are today?

- Do you have recurring dreams that haunt you or delight you, dreams that communicate something of your future treasure?

## What is Your Personal Legend?

*"It's what you've always wanted to accomplish. Everyone, when they are young, knows what their Personal Legend is."* (p. 21)

*"…that desire originated in the soul of the universe."* (p. 22)

*"And, when you want something, all the universe conspires in helping you achieve it."* (p. 22)

Santiago meets a mysterious man in Tarifa who knows very specific information about Santiago's past. Santiago is convinced the man is a wizard or mage.

The man claims to be King Melchizedek—the word in Hebrew translates to "my king (is) righteous(ness)."

> *"It's a force that appears to be negative, but actually shows you how to realize your Personal Legend. It prepares your spirit and your will, because there is one great truth on this planet: whoever you are, or whatever it is that you do, when you really want something, it's because that desire originated in the soul of the universe. It's your mission on earth."* (p. 22)

> *"The Soul of the World is nourished by people's happiness. And also by unhappiness, envy, and jealousy. To realize one's Personal Legend is a person's only real obligation. All things are one."* (p. 22)

**Uncovering your Personal Legend**

(Based on Coelho's definition: a Personal Legend is something that you've always wanted to accomplish. It's a desire to do and be something that has attracted you throughout your lifetime and that has brought you to this moment. It's your mission on earth.)

Set your timer for fifteen to twenty minutes:

- What have you wanted to do or be the most since childhood? (Your first glimpse at your Personal Legend.)

- How has your life supported (even at times when you felt it thwarted) your journey to become and live your Personal Legend?

- Are you living your Personal Legend now?

This next question is a big one and I'd like you to riff on it for **ten minutes**. GO!

**If your only REAL obligation was to realize your Personal Legend, how would you change your business, your brand and your life?**

## Detours on the Way to Bliss

*"He realized that he had to choose between thinking of himself as the poor victim of a thief or as an adventurer in quest of his treasure.*

*I am an adventurer."* (p. 42)

Just before Part 2 of *The Alchemist*, Santiago's small fortune for selling his sheep to King Melchizedek is stolen by the con man he has entrusted to take him to the pyramids to find his treasure.

He can choose to give up on his dream or he can surrender to his Personal Legend.

Take a **twenty-five minute** dream detour and riff on these prompts:

- Have you ever felt "taken in" or tricked or conned by someone you trusted?

- Have you ever felt so discouraged in your business that you wanted to give up and go in another direction?

- What helped you stay on the path?

Santiago sleeps all night in the middle of the marketplace, without any food, friends, family or a penny in his pocket. He wakes up feeling happy, having decided to follow his dream and find his treasure. A merchant in the market gives him a smile and a piece of candy.

To make money, have a place to live and food to eat, Santiago begins to work for a glass merchant in a shop at the top of the hill. With Santiago's help, his new employer sells more glasses and makes more money. After one year Santiago has saved enough money to travel on to the Egyptian pyramids to realize his Personal Legend.

"You must always know what it is that you want," the old king had told him."

But before Santiago leaves the glass shop, he must decide whether to go back to his homeland and buy a new flock of sheep or move forward with his dream to travel to the Pyramids and find his treasure.

As he walks out the door he remembers the smile on the candy seller's face when he had no food or a place to go. He remembers that the king had the same smile. Santiago puts his hand in his pockets and feels his Urim and Thummim divination stones given to him by King Melchizedek.

They connect him to the king's strength and he chooses to keep following the path to his dream.

**Do we need to give up love or a love partnership to realize our Personal Legend?**

Santiago makes the trek across the desert to reach the oasis Al Fayoum in Egypt where he meets Fatima, a Bedouin woman. He falls in love at first sight and wants to stay with her rather than leave to go to the pyramids. He thinks that she is his treasure.

"You have told me about your dreams… I am a part of your dream, a part of your Personal Legend, as you call it.

That's why I want you to continue toward your goal." (p. 97)

As difficult as it is for Santiago to leave Fatima behind, he knows she is right. He continues on with her blessing and the alchemist's blessing as well.

- Who are your allies and helping forces—those who rush to your side to help you keep going forward on your path?

- How have detours help you clarify your dream and your Personal Legend?

**Following the Signs + Omens**

Throughout *The Alchemist*, signs and omens direct Santiago to exactly where he needs to go to realize his Personal Legend.

When I get a "hit" or a "sign" that the time is right or wrong, I do my best to follow through, listening to my intuition. However there were times when I've ignored those feelings and signs and ended up in situations that were difficult or challenging. Stay extra alert and pay attention to signs that are both subtle and obvious.

Keep a record of everything you notice and all of the synchronicities. The more you notice the more you'll see.

**Ways You Can Receive Signs/Omens Connected to Your Personal Legend:**

1. Phone calls or emails out of the blue that contain the perfect advice or information, or even an offer of help from someone.

2. Animals that point us in the direction of our dreams! Look for animal allies that show up when you're thinking about your dreams or after you've asked for help or information. A great website to check out animal meanings is www.whats-your-sign.com/animal-totems.html.

3. Songs on the radio with lyrics that speak to you and your Personal Legend.

4. Books that fall off the shelf or when your eye is drawn to a particular title or cover and you open to a page where the text answers your question, helps solve a problem or contains a special message.

5. You overhear a conversation, possibly between total strangers, but the message is totally meant for you!

6. You are drawn to a piece of visual art and then realize its title or theme is directly answering a prayer or pointing you in the direction of your Personal Legend.

   *"...intuition is really a sudden immersion of the soul into the universal current of life..."* (p. 74)

**Spend ten minutes making a list of signs you received in the past year that helped you realize your Personal Legend.**

**How did each decision feel to you at first? (labels like crazy, wrong, right on target, exciting, scary, strengthening, adventurous, courageous are a small sample of common feelings.)**

**Spend another five minutes thinking back to when you started the most current incarnation of your business? Did similar decisions come up then? Were the results of your decisions different?**

Sidenote: You may have noticed that *The Alchemist* corresponds to the patterns of Joseph Campbell's *Hero's Journey*.

Even more noticeable to me is how Santiago's journey is similar to our own entrepreneurial odysseys. The story portrays three stages of a pilgrimage:

1. The Beginning :: Ease and Beginner's Luck.

   We feel lucky and energized that we found our purpose in life. Our excitement and enthusiasm are naturally high at this time. And what attracts clients like bees to honey? Excitement, high energy and enthusiasm, of course!

2. The Middle :: Trials and Detours.

   During the middle of a journey we are tested to see if we can be tempted off the path to our Personal Legends. We fall on our butts many times, but stand back up and brush off the dirt. We keep moving forward as if something is pulling us along.

3. The End :: Final Test and Recovering the Treasure.

   Near the end of the journey, when we are ready to completely give up, extra courage and stamina are needed. There is usually one major test at this point to see if we indeed have the fortitude to stay the path. For Santiago, this is when he gets to the pyramids and is nearly beaten to death by the man who unknowingly tells him exactly where to find his treasure!

Where are you now in your own business?. Which stage of the journey are you on? I believe that we cycle through the three stages multiple times in the evolution of our brand.

Spend **twenty minutes** writing about the stage you're currently experiencing.

- Brainstorm! What's going on, who's in the scene with you, where are you, what kind of decisions are you making and what overall feelings are you experiencing?

- If there's an extra minute or two, think of experiences you've lived through then mark the other two stages you aren't currently working through.

## Let Your Heart Guide Your Actions

*"Listen to your heart. It knows all things, because it came from the Soul of the World, and it will one day return there."* (p. 127)

We left off as Santiago was traveling through the war torn Sahara desert with the alchemist in search of his treasure at the pyramids.

He left behind the love of his life, the safety of the oasis and gave up the small fortune he'd built up AGAIN—all to realize his Personal Legend.

After giving up worldly things and the familiar paths he paved, his heart begins to whisper more loudly. The universe truly conspires to help him now that he has proven to his soul that he intends to see his Personal Legend through to the end and that he will always listen to his heart.

Take **thirty minutes** to meditate: listen to the voice of your heart.

**When was the last time you had a conversation with your heart?**

**Maybe so long ago that you don't recognize its voice.**

**Try this as a daily practice for at least three days this week and journal out the conversation, messages and images after each sitting.**

**Do this in your car, sitting in a park, while walking on the beach or to work, in a yoga pose (I find it's often easier to hear my heart's voice while moving):**

1. Ask your heart to come forward and tell you anything that it longs to. Just listen. No judgement. No interrupting or arguing either.

2. When you hear a message write it down.

3. Ask your heart one question, or two. A question that's really burning within you. Write down the answer you are given.

4. Thank your heart.

5. Commit to your heart. Tell it that you will listen to it from now on and take action as needed.

6. Write down at least one small action step you can take to heed the advice of your heart.

7. Do it!

Notice how you begin to feel after 48 hours of making conscious connection with your heart. Most of my clients report feelings of bliss, calm, excitement, discovery and centeredness.

Obviously, the more you do this the better you will feel. Don't limit your heart conversations to just once a day or for only these two days.

## Create Content in Alignment With Your Mythic Brand

Earlier in this book, in Chapter 1 to be exact, you began the inquiry into your *mythic brand*. It's the brand behind your brand, or it can be a whole new world you create to flow in to as you move into the new year.

Read your notes about your brand model and description, its style and tone and what you long to express through your brand. **Take thirty minutes** to review and then answer the prompt below. I'd especially like you to brainstorm a list of potential content that sounds like fun to YOU.

**What kinds of programs, blog posts, newsletter, videos, podcasts... engaging, binge-worthy content would feel delicious for you to deliver to your audience?**

All content you create holds the flavor, the energy and intention of your brand.

If you feel stressed, exhausted, burnt-out, bored or frustrated when you're creating branded content, guess what? That energy will come through to those who engage with your work.

The prime objective of creating a mythic brand is to engage your IMAGINATION.

The second, which is 100% connected to the prime objective, is to feel and express PLEASURE so you can be your best self in your work.

**Brand Awareness + Connection to your Personal Legend**

> *"There is only one way to learn," the alchemist answered. "It's through action. Everything you need to know you have learned through your journey."* (p. 125)

Here the Alchemist is referring to the fact that we just can't KNOW what our Personal Legend is, we have to take action and live it.

Meet it out in the world and give expression to it.

You've been on your journey to realize your Personal Legend since the day you were born.

So far in this chapter, you reviewed your dreams from childhood and your current longings; you've written about your journey and where you believe you are now. At this point, you are walking on the road—becoming even more connected to your destiny, your Personal Legend.

It's time to connect the journey, the trials and learnings and the triumphs, everything you've experienced in your life... to your brand.

> *"You've got to find the treasure, so that everything you have learned along the way can make sense."* (p. 116)

Your treasure = your destiny fulfilled.

**And interestingly:**

Your brand = your life experience + destiny fulfilled.

The right images, colors, design and copy for your company or personal brand *do not* come before doing this work. All of the outer elements come after the testing of your soul—after listening to your heart and taking action, even when the path is fogged over and covered with a dense jungle.

As you refine your life, your brand will follow. It's an organic process.

Your treasure revolves around a particular set of themes that weave through your life.

When you create a website or finish a book you feel fulfilled, for a while. Complete. And you celebrate.

After a time, you will feel drawn to new projects or experiences; these become your "new" treasure.

There is nothing wrong with this! It's the cyclical nature of life. Your brand will evolve over time.

When you see a stellar + inspiring brand, you don't necessarily see the pain and love and sweat and joy that went into creating it. You are seeing the results of it ALL.

A brand that becomes worshipped and adored feels like the be all, end all. In the past I believed that too.

It's not. It's only the beginning.

Your brand IS mythic. You DEFINE your Personal Legend then clothe it in messaging and colors that speak authentically from your heart to others in the outer world. We make choices when we create art, commit to it and put it out in the world. After it is received, we refine and revise it as needed. The process is fluid.

Your brand reaches for its ultimate destination; but it never stops moving toward it. We can see an example of this process in the story of the god Dionysus. He is always seeking the home he never finds. This is because home, aka the treasure, is only found in the heart and in response to the soul's yearnings.

Take **one hour** to answer these brand mapping prompts—if you don't finish them all in one day spread them out. Take as much time as you need to get through all of them:

1. The themes that have woven their way through my life (such as leadership, mentoring, teaching, conflict with authority, love, death/rebirth, etc.) are. [Create a list that feels full and complete.]

2. Right now I'm in the [beginning/middle/end] of my current journey to find my treasure.

3. Certain stories + experiences repeat over and over again in my life. The one that has the most relevance to me TODAY is... [Describe the *one* story that grabs you the most at present.]

4. My Personal Legend centers around the themes, stories and experiences I wrote about in prompts #1 and #3 above. Therefore, at this time my Personal Legend is all about . [What are you teaching people about? What are you always going on and on about? What keeps you awake at night? What do you stand up for?]

5. Is there a particular archetype, god, goddess, idea, concept or well-known personality that encapsulates the qualities of your Personal Legend? If so, who or what? [Make a list that feels whole and complete to you; you can list multiple influences.]

6. Search for clues in your obsessions and passions. What's going on in the world, in pop culture, in your neighborhood that has captured your attention?

7. If your brand had an animal totem, which would it be? [look to your favorite animal allies in dreams and life. also check out this website for inspiration.]

8.  What form does your service take? Name the qualities and see how they connect to your life stories and the themes you called out in prompts #1- #4 above.

9.  What do you love doing? What energizes you?

10. You were born to give your gift. How will you deliver that baby in a way that honors the attributes of your brand as defined in the first nine prompts? [Check your list from last week's prompt: What kinds of programs, concerts, art exhibits, pop-up poetry reading, open mic night, blog posts, newsletter, videos, podcasts, dance parties, high tea, retreats, workshops... engaging, binge-worthy content would feel delicious for you to deliver to your audience?]

Take **one hour to work these final prompts** - if you don't finish them all in one day spread them out. Take as much time as you need to get through everything:

1.  In one sentence write what you LOVE about your brand.

2.  In one sentence write WHY you do your work in the world.

3.  Decide on three to five easy action steps you will take in the next 48 hours to use something profound you've learned about in this chapter to upgrade your brand.

I think I'll let you rest for now.

You did some major heavy lifting. Your muscles may feel a little sore, but that good kind of ache is what we're going for.

I'm in love with branding because it's a rich process. It's fun. It's a challenge.

And when we go with our hearts and our intuition everything FLOWS.

# Interview: Alexandra Franzen

*I am so honored and elated to be interviewing an entrepreneurial luminary of our time, Alexandra Franzen. She has so much incredible depth when you work with her in a workshop, she acts as a midwife. She has this potent magic to help you birth the person, the self that you are becoming, that maybe you only had glimmers of previously.*

Oh, thank you. What a tremendous introduction. I feel awash in splendor.

*What was the breakthrough moment for you in your career when you just knew that wow, this has been a huge opening? Something is really happening. You know, the heavens open up and the angels sing and then you sing, "Hallelujah!"*

A breakthrough moment. There have been a lot, but I would say one that jumps to mind was the very, very first time that I sent out a poll to my blog readers and subscribers asking them to tell *me* what they thought of me. I gave people some very specific prompts and questions 'cause I was really trying to see. I think I know who I am and I think I know how my writing and my work is resonating in the world, but you never really know. Until you ask people, you know, why do you read my stuff? What keeps you coming back? And what is this doing for you?

What was so fascinating to me was that the types of responses I got had nothing to do with marketing or branding, or self-promotion, or copywriting, or even business. None of the responses had anything to do with what I thought my job was. And, in fact, the—sort of the prevailing sentiment that people wrote back to me was, "When I read your stuff, I feel like you're talking to me and I feel like what I want is possible."

And that was a breakthrough moment because it, it made me see myself more clearly and it made me realize, Wait! That's what I want. Like that's actually the point of all of this, and it allowed to me start writing and tailoring myself even more in that direction.

So, side note. If you've never polled or surveyed your readers, or even your friends, to find out what they see in you and why they come to you, it's an invaluable exercise. It just takes a few minutes and an email to do.

*Very, very wise. I mean, it seems like kind of the obvious thing: ask people. Ask our readers, so few of us do that. So, thank you for that.*

*So, what activities do you use to build your Twitter following, as you know as strong as it is, and also your subscriber base? Do you have any special strategies or tactics?*

Hmm, you know it's funny because I'm sort of like the anti-tactic approach in that I don't have a content calendar, I don't have like marketing milestones. I never ever have said, "I'm going to Tweet three times a day about these topics, doot-doot-doot and then suddenly, like people will materialize and fall in love with me and everything is going to be great." I just can't do that. It just doesn't sit well with me. So what I always strive to do is to write and release content into the world what I deem consistently. Which for me means about two times a week.

I will release a new blog post, a new something for people to see and I'll send that out to my mailing list and I'll post it on my blog. Simple. It's not every Tuesday, it's not every Friday. It's when I feel inspired to write something and I think that my audience is cool with that, and I've actually had people say to me I like the fact that sometimes you send a newsletter at 11 PM on Saturday night, which is a marketing "no-no" but it feels authentic because they know I just wrote it right then in that moment. So, there's something to be said for breaking the rules.

I view Twitter as a mini version of my blog, where I can be a little more personal, a little more quirky, a little more non sequitur. And as long as what I'm tweeting feels either informative or entertaining, or insightful or inspiring, it kind of doesn't matter what it is because it will either resonate with people or it won't.

So my philosophy is to be relatively consistent, to write when you feel inspired to write, and just make sure whatever you are putting out there is either informative or inspiring, or insightful or entertaining, or some combination thereof. And that's really the nuts and bolts of my whole strategy.

One technique (I prefer the word technique to tactic because it's not a war or something.) One technique that I've started to employ this year, which I didn't really do before, is to end my blog posts with a prompt, with a question, with something to spark discussion. Not something cheesy, like "so what do you think guys?"

But it's a genuine question that takes the theme of my posts and turns it into a conversation. Once I made that connection, I noticed that I started to get a lot more comments. Whereas before people might Tweet or share my posts on Facebook but they weren't really commenting because I didn't really leave the door open for any comments to happen.

*You're inviting dialogue. So that they're a part of your world and you're a part of theirs. That's wonderful.*

This is a personal revelation, but I think that in the past I was resistant to inviting dialogue on my site because I didn't want to be a community manager and I didn't want to be a camp mom and I felt very strapped for time. It just felt like one more thing to have to moderate but as my business and my life evolves toward more space and I start feeling more generous, then I want the door to be propped open and I want the discussion to happen, and it feels easy. So, I think there are times in your life and your business where you just aren't even thinking in terms of community and other times when it's exciting. So it's interesting to notice that about yourself.

*What is your magical mojo secret around having such a long waiting list? (I'm referencing her former service Velocity, which*

*Alexandra no longer offers.) And how did it happen for you? How did you make it happen?*

I've often wondered myself how this happened and I think if I look back at the different pieces in the story about how I created this offering and started promoting it and how the first round of people came, up to today where I'm essentially booked a year in advance. I think there's a couple things at play. The first is that as a copywriter, I made a very deliberate decision to repackage myself in a way that was completely unlike what pretty much all of my peers were doing. So, rather than positioning myself as a copywriter who is going to work with you over the course of 10 hours or 20 hours or a month or whatever, to write your web copy and your newsletters, etc., etc. I positioned that same stuff as a day that's an immersive, lightning bolt experience. Truly a once-in-a-lifetime or maybe twice-in-a-lifetime experience that you're going to emerge from transformed.

I think people don't like to have to wait a month to see their web copy. They like things done right away and I knew that I would be able to deliver on that promise. So, that's #1 is just that the packaging of it and the energy of it is very different than what I think a lot of people see when they're looking to hire a writer, or a copywriter, or a scribe. The other thing is that my personal business credo is under-promise and over-deliver. So I made it very intentional, I under-promise. You know, I don't really talk about the fact that it's kind of like a spiritual experience for some people. I don't promise that I'm going to write a book for you. I make promises that I know I can keep or even more than keep. That way people leave feeling delighted and awestruck instead of feeling like yeah, well, I really wish we had gotten to x, y, and z. So, under-promise, over-deliver, very-very solid strategy for being very booked and very busy. [laughs]

The other piece is that, you know, and I don't really know how to describe this, but again, when somebody is shopping around for say graphic designer or web designer, or copywriter or business coach, I think more and more people are less motivated by the sales copy on your website and more motivated by how they feel when they meet you online:

*How do they feel when they're reading your blog, looking at your videos, experiencing all of your stuff? And I think that I've been able to successfully create an experience on my website that the right people just love and when people find me and they resonate with me. People have said this to me, I'm not making this up.*

They will write to me and say, "I don't care if I have to wait 10 months to work with you. I only want to work with you." And the first couple of times I got that email I wanted to say "but you realize there are hundreds of writers who can do what I do" and "please, here's my favorite, go hire one of them." And they will literally say, "No. Put me on your waiting list. I want to wait."

So, there's something about finding the right teacher at the right moment, or finding the right creative partner at the right moment, where you just know in your heart of hearts, this is the one I want and I am happy to be patient, I am happy to wait for the real thing. And I feel that sometimes when I find people online. So, I think I've been able to cultivate a presence that allows for that kind of connection to happen. Where people are willing to wait.

Fourth thing, lots of pieces here. Fourth, and last thing is I don't give you any other option. Right? There's no mini package so you either wait or you don't. And I think that *that*, more than anything else, has been the secret to my success with this. Because there's no flimsiness and no wobbliness.

*I love that. I know and it's hard to pare down your offerings. I think as entrepreneurs, we throw the spaghetti at the wall and see what fits for a while and then what works and what doesn't work.*

Having just one service, of course, is not the correct or the best solution for every entrepreneur, but it's worth experimenting with. Especially if you're feeling a little bit fragmented and scattered and overwhelmed.

A good parallel might be if you think of Placido Domingo, world-class opera singer, completely legendary. The best, the top in his field. He doesn't do one song at a random show and then run across town to do a little bit over here. You book him for a legendary evening and that's it. Know what I mean?

So, not that you want to overblow your ego but if you think about yourself as wanting to be truly a legendary service provider or entrepreneur in your field. How do you want to be treated? How should people be able to access and book you? In little chunks?

Or in one big immersive, transformative experience? It's worth considering.

### Can you tell us a little bit about your books and how you got into your publishing deals and your literary agent?

Yes, absolutely. I am just so excited to be a published author. It's been a lifelong dream and it still doesn't really feel real. Even though both of the manuscripts are delivered and it's happening, I still can't really believe it. But, you know, the way that this all came about is the way that most things come about in life, through relationships and through sort of side door synchronicity. I received an email, maybe a year ago, from a literary agent who is a lovely woman living in Boulder, Colorado. She had been in the business for eleven or twelve years and she was looking for a copywriter to help write her web copy. And I helped her with that, and we, you know, organically sprung up sort of an online friendship and I think at some point in our email chatter she asked if I had any book projects I had ever considering doing and of course, I said "do I ever! How much time do you have?" And this began kind of a back and forth flow of ideas and she helped me to refine some of them. And at one point we got on the phone and kind of had like the official conversation where she said, "I think this idea is solid and I want you to do a proposal, you know, I'll start shopping it around." And somehow, just like that I had a literary agent.

So, again, you know, it wasn't me querying people, it wasn't a total miracle. It came out of a relationship that happened because of my presence and who I am and the work that I do online. And the way that I wound up with two book projects is kinda funny. We pitched my proposal for *50 Ways to Say You're Awesome* and pretty quickly had an offer on the table, which was really mind-blowingly exciting. But what happened was when my agent pitched the book to Potter Style, which is an imprint of Random House Crown, they basically said, this is really cute. It's not really for us, you know, we don't see it fitting with our collection. But we've got this other project, we're looking for a contributing writer, would Alexandra be interested?

*I am so elated for you. That's so inspiring and beautiful.*

Yeah, as with many things in my life, there's no magic secret to how it happened. Not that I'm an expert on the publishing industry by any means, but I will say that for people who are wanting to get into publishing, like traditional print publishing, and this is very common knowledge. Now more than ever publishers and agents are looking for people who have a platform. Online. And a platform doesn't just mean that you have a large audience or a huge following. You don't necessarily have to have bajillions and jillions of subscribers and followers. A platform really means that you have a clear message you're standing on that's distinct and identifiable, that people could recognize. And if you happen to have a significant audience, all the better. But it's also about your connections. It's about people in your network that you can leverage. But really the main thing is do you have that clear identifiable message where when somebody Googles you it's evident what you stand for, why you do it? And the people who are around you. That's really what publishers are looking for.

It's not enough just to have a great idea. You have to have sort of proven that you're invested in that idea, that it's your life.

*Any advice for new and upcoming or up and coming entrepreneurs?*

New and up and coming entrepreneurs. Hmmm. You know, I'll just reiterate what I said earlier about my own work and my own Velocity sessions. If you can under-promise and over-deliver every time with great devotion and consistency, I promise you cannot fail. And you will delight people and they will not be able to stop talking about you. Which will lead to immensely organic marketing and client attraction that requires no hustling and no sleaziness and no force. So again, under-promise, over-deliver, make it easy for people to be delighted by you. You will be very, very successful and rewarded.

*Perfect.*

The end.

# Meditation + Breathwork

**Focus**: Chakra 1, Root (located at perineum)

**Sanskrit**: Muladhara, root

**Associations**: Survival, Stability, Grounding, Home, Family, Prosperity, Right Livelihood, Health, Matter, Earthly Realm and Lotus Growing from the Mud

**Planet**: Saturn

**Day of the Week**: Saturday

**Archetypes**: Gaia, Cronos/Saturn, Rhea, Pachamama, Hera, Cybele, Geb, Enki, Dionysus, Demeter

We have arrived home at our base chakra, the root chakra, known as *muladhara* in Sanskrit.

Muladhara is the seat of kundalini Shakti, the serpentine, feminine life force that awaits "arousal." This chakra is located near the basal end of the spinal column in the vicinity of the coccygeal plexus beneath the sacrumit. Its kshetram, or superficial activation point, is located on the perineum.

Its symbol is a yellow, square lotus, surrounded by eight shining spears on the sides and corners with four red petals. The deity of this region is Indra, who is yellow in color, four-armed, holding a vajra and blue lotus in his hands. He is mounted upon the white elephant Airavata, who has seven trunks, denoting the seven elements vital to physical functioning. Occasionally, instead of Indra, the deity may be Ganesha, with coral orange skin, wearing a lemon yellow dhoti with a green silk scarf draped around his shoulders. In three hands he holds a ladoo, a lotus flower and a hatchet, and the fourth is raised in the mudra dispelling fear.

The number seven again holds symbolic power over us, as this chakra holds infinite potential.

Weaving your way through each chapter, you worked downwards from the higher level chakras, taking the manifesting path. My intention is to bring Cosmic energies down into our lived realities.

Practice breathing directly through the four, downward facing petals of the root chakra, directing the energy upwards, directly to the upward facing 1,000 petaled lotus of the crown chakra.

Focus on clearing your prana tube, the channel of energy that runs from your crown chakra all the way down to your base chakra. As you move the energy down from the crown see it unblock and energize each chakra as it travels.

Then reverse the flow and bring the energy up from the root, bathing all the chakras as it travels to the crown chakra at the top of your head.

Do three repetitions in each direction and always end the practice by moving energy down from the crown chakra to the base chakra and root into the core of the earth.

When you open yourself to Divine Source... and then vision, speak, imagine, love and create that energy into existence, you are the Magician.

You carry the seed for the Music of the Spheres in your DNA.

We know the facts: we are all one heart beating, we are always connected to the Divine and what we create out of this energy is infinite.

Malkuth, which means *kingdom*, is the name of this final spiritual center found at the roots of the Tree of Live. The other name for Malkuth is SHEKINAH, which means "dwelling" and is considered the feminine aspect of God in Judaism. Often this center is symbolized by the image of a bride.

## Body Prayer

What is the temple (or temples) where the Divine YOU can reside? Boldly claim your space : Your home : Yourself as the Divine Creator in your life.

Settle in.

Think of one moment in your life when you felt completely in your element.

What were you doing? Thinking? Feeling?

Write down one sentence or one word that encapsulates that moment.

Now translate the words into body movement. Turn on your favorite music and begin creating shapes and poses with your body that express that blissful time.

**Journaling Prompts:**

What is the legacy you are building through your work?

# Chapter 8: Shadow Play

*"To be wounded is to be opened to the world; it is to be pushed off the straight, fixed and predictable path of certainty and thrown into ambiguity, or onto the circuitous path, and into the unseen and unforeseen."*

**–Dennis Patrick Slattery,** *The Wounded Body*

Get ready to release your Shadow and PLAY!

We are the change agents. We are dynamic + courageous… wild. Sexy. Transparent. Magical.

We want to shine, be ourselves + attract the clients, contracts and customers that will support our lifestyles.

And, this is exactly where we begin to play small, hesitate and draw back our power and light. The vulnerability we feel at being seen and heard is normal and real… and completely debilitating at times.

The two biggest fears for entrepreneurs are:

- Fear of being invisible
- Fear of being seen

Like many contradictions we encounter throughout our lives, the meeting of two opposite fears or states of being is the place where we discover our superpowers. Where the light meets the dark is the space of greatest potential.

Looking for your gifts in the light yields only 10-20% of your potential power. Like the submerged part of an iceberg, the unknown and unconscious aspects of ourselves make up the majority of our consciousness.

The Shadow does not want to have the light cast on it, however it desires a voice and a body.

**Before we dive into our Shadow play, I want to give you the lay of the land.**

# Attributes of The Shadow: The Landscape of the Repressed + Hidden

**Quick factoids about our Shadows (adapted from Vogler's book** *The Writer's Journey*)**:**

- Represent the energy of the unexpressed, repressed and rejected aspects of something; it can be both negative and positive.

- Hide or deny emotions that can turn ugly and destructive.

- In dreams may appear as monsters; many are also shapeshifters, such as wizards, witches, selkies, werewolves or animal guides.

- Challenge the Hero and give her or him a worthy opponent. The Hero/ine in you is the Ego. A healthy ego is needed to dialogue with the Shadow and, maintain compassion for your Shadow self. This aspect of you IS NOT a dragon to be slayed!

- Create conflict and life-threatening situations in stories. In our psyche, shadows can make us feel like something is life-threatening when it's really not.

- Have a touch of goodness and a vulnerable side to humanize them.

- Do not think of themselves as villains; from their point of view they are the Hero of their own myth. The audience's Hero is their villain. (How's that for a twist?)

- May represent unexplored potential, creativity, "the roads not taken"—the possibilities of life that we eliminate by making choices at various stages

- Sometimes appear as the "Inner Critic" or "Sabateur."

- May appear as a neglected or abandoned Child.

The variations are numerous, but basically any part of you that you don't or can't express openly becomes part of your Shadow self.

As you do Shadow work, your compassion, passion and love for your clients and audience will grow into a serious love fest!

The relationship with our customers should be a LOVE FEST. As you feel more love and compassion towards your clients, they will begin to crave you and your offerings and you'll begin to LUST after them with abandon! A mutually beneficial situation, yes?

# Your Supernaturally Designed Client (SDC)

Build a trusting, loving and lasting relationship with the customers you crave.

Architect your ideal customer. Since "ideal client" and "client avatar" are overused and totally impersonal. I thought I would offer a new terminology and approach.

Design. Your. Client.

Don't you love it when someone creates the perfect service, like a coaching program or a workshop that seems to have been designed specifically just for you? Don't you wonder if someone crawled into your head... and telepathically picked up on your problem?

You too can be someone's answered prayer.

**Part 1: The Basics**

Step 1. Make a list of specific problems your SDC (supernaturally designed client) has in relation to your most prized skills, talents and expertise.

Step 2. Which of these problems needs solving ASAP?

(Choose one or two problems to focus on for now.)

Step 3. Is there are problem that comes up again and again? What didn't work to help them initiate lasting change?

Step 4. What do they want so badly that they'd invest as much of their hard-earned money as possible?

**Part 2: A Day in the Life**

Enter an imaginal, playful state and begin breathing life into your character.

You can survey or interview a current SDC to obtain real life data.

However, I find that my imagination/intuition usually paints an accurate picture.

Give your SDC description plenty of vivid details.

- What does your SDC's ordinary Monday look like? Start from the morning all the way until their head hits the pillow. Do they drink coffee or tea? Eggs sunny side up or poached? You get the picture…

- How about an ordinary weekend?

- How do they feel about orgasms?

- What do they order in a restaurant?

- What is their fantasy vacation? Where would they go? What would they do?

- What would be their dreamiest day ever? A day when they felt the happiest and most relaxed ever.

- What do they loathe?

- What do they run away from?

**Part 3: Write a full o' juicy details character sketch of your SDC.**

Using the information you've channeled and/or gleaned, write a short scene where your SDC is dealing with the problem that you can help solve. Choose any genre/style you want. Have fun!

Introduce them into the scene as if they're walking on stage or screen for the first time. Describe their situation before they find you. Describe how they find you and what it's like for them to work with you. End by describing their world after you've helped them solve their problem.

**Here's my character sketch for an SDC named Skye:**

*Another workshop with no sign-ups. Only 2 days left until the deadline.*

*Skye feels despondent. She usually has at least 10 people sign up for a workshop, but now there's not a single peep from her 300 member newsletter list.*

*Over the past 5 months her numbers have dwindled. Open and click rates are wayyyy down from where they were last quarter. Even when Skye offers up her time for FREE, still nothing. Just crickets.*

*"People just don't want what I have to give."*

*Skye goes to the kitchen to make something to eat. She is 27 years old and has a lovely apartment, but not much happening in the kitchen (or the bedroom for that matter).*

*"I could use an orgasm right about now." She thinks looking at the drawer with her vibrator in it; but that just isn't cutting it anymore. Skye wants a warm body next to her in the bed. Her cat jumps up next to her and sleekly snuggles past. "Not you, Mr. Big. I think it's time to have a real man around the house." (Her cat knows not to take offense at her remark. His name was inspired by Carrie Bradshaw's boyfriend in Sex and the City, one of her guilty pleasures.)*

*She feels like her life has turned to sludge. Her body feels so heavy in the morning that she can barely get out of bed.*

*"How am I going to pay the bills? Keep this place?" The thought of moving in with her parents makes her shudder. She's so preoccupied that she forgets to eat. "Fuck it," she thinks to herself.*

*"Fuck the world. No, fuck ME. I can't figure out how to get people to pay for anything. They run off to Goddess Leonie, Marie Forleo's B-School, what's-her-name's social media bootcamp—for THOUSANDS OF DOLLARS! They have money to spend, so why don't they buy from ME?"*

*"I've got to do something before I go mad." Skye takes a quick run around the block. The movement gets her out of her slump.*

*"OK. I can handle this. It's green smoothie time."*

*She takes a deep breath or two, makes her smoothie and sits down to watch her favorite show,* Lost Girl.

*After that she does a little work on her upcoming self-help book (in the works for about six months now) about how to overcome your blocks to financial freedom and live a life of joy and abundance.*

*And, then the idea hits her. "I should do this book as a workshop first. It would help so many people and I would loooove teaching it." She realizes that she needs caffeine-inspiration so she heads down the street to her favorite pumpkin-spice latte dispensary with her laptop in tow.*

*As she sits down to her sweet steaming treat, her mail program bleeps and an email from one of her favorite peeps, Kris Oster [yay me!] pops into her window.*

*"Ah, wonder what the Mermaid Chick has for me today." She thinks excitedly as she clicks on the email to see what it's all about.*

*The email is a revelation! It's exactly what she needs to hear and learn. With this knowledge and Kris' guidance she'll sell out this new workshop in a few days. She can feel it in her bones. Her body feels electric, alive. Skye knows she is ready to step up and have even more customers.*

*She sees the light at the end of her dark tunnel, her dead stagnant body is reanimated.*

*"I have got to sign up for this!!!"*

[After she takes my workshop...]

*Skye drafts a sales love letter to go out to her list of 300. Her sales page is polished and her PayPal account is at the ready. She's proud of her offering and proud that she didn't give up on herself again—proud that she has moved through her fear of rejection and gotten her work out there. Ultimately, she knows she is on the planet to be of service to thousands of women. She feels supported by Kris and the tribe on the workshop that Facebook group is rallying around here.*

*"I have nothing to lose. I've got this."*

*Skye hits the "Send" button on MailChimp. Deep breath.*

*She sees the numbers go up for the sign ups that start dribbling in about 5 minutes after she sends the email. First 10 signups come fast and furious... than another 5 or 6. Then the next day another 7 or 8, and then 5 the last day. She sees 20, no 30 signups for her workshop and the numbers of her bank account are going up too.*

*She jumps up and down excitedly. She tells everyone about it on FB group.*

*Tears of happiness on her face, she's glowing and radiant. "You rock!" She says to her reflection in the mirror and she looks up towards her angels and guides in the heavens and utters a sincere, heartfelt, "Thank you."*

*She celebrates by having a True Blood marathon with her besties and rewards herself with a spa pedicure.*

*Skye feels peaceful, fulfilled and relaxed in her skin. Her trust in herself and in the universe is restored. All is well.*

# Sleeping Beauty ... Dreaming in the Darkness

*"We find that by opening the door to the shadow realm a little, and letting out various elements a few at a time, relating to them, finding use for them, negotiating, we can reduce being surprised by shadow sneak attacks and unexpected explosions."*

–Clarissa Pinkola Estés, *Women Who Run With the Wolves: Myths and Stories of the Wild Woman Archetype*

## The Journey to the Underworld

The most famous journey-to-the-underworld myths are the Descent of Inanna, The Tale of Psyche and Eros, and Persephone's abduction into Hades. The journey to the underworld and the ascent back up to the light world is a myth of initiation, death and rebirth.

The underworld journey is a dangerous face-off with the forces of Death. The sleeping death that we see highlighted in many fairy tales has deep roots in the archetypal journey into the underworld. It is a calculated or intended dip under the surface of consciousness.

The sleeping princess in fairy tales is the archetypal representation of the feminine alchemical vessel for transformation. Just as a caterpillar spins its cocoon and then completely transforms in the dark stillness, when we stop doing and go into deeper places within, we awaken to our new form as a butterfly.

Sleeping Beauty, Snow White and Psyche at the surface seem rather dull to our contemporary mindset, which posits that heroines need to be warriors, freedom fighters or movers and shakers to change the world. I wish to reclaim the Sleeping Princess as an archetype of transformation for both women and men. This may feel frightening at first because stillness and darkness are equated with the Death archetype in our psyches. Complete chaos, loss of control and surrender are trying tests for the egoic Hero or Heroine within.

When one thinks of complete surrender to death and resurrection, numerous figures come to mind: Osiris, Jesus, Odin, Dionysus and Persephone.

# Mythic Associations: The Dark Goddess–Guardians of Death, Transformation and Regeneration

There are two versions of the Persephone/Demeter stories. The classical, post-patriarchal Greco-Roman myth states that Persephone/Proserpine was abducted and raped by Hades/Pluto (Greek/Roman) and dragged to the underworld forcibly against her will. In Charlene Spretnak's retelling, from the book *Lost Goddesses of Early Greece: A Collection of Pre-Hellenic Myths*, we get a completely different story: Persephone wants to help the souls of the dead who are lost and living in darkness. She makes a conscious choice to be of service and descends to Hades, even though her mother Demeter wishes she would stay above the ground.

**Journaling Prompts:**

What part of you is dying to be reborn? What aspect of your business/livelihood is dying away, making room for new birth?

In your own life, when have you felt that you were forced by fate, destiny or circumstances beyond your control to descend to the underworld?

(Some examples: physical or mental illness; depression; difficult relationship; marriage, money or career experience; or death of a beloved family member, friend or pet.)

Write down the details of the experience.

Now, re-write the situation as if you were the Persephone in Spretnak's retelling of the Persephone myth.

**How would you revision the situation to respond to the circumstances from an empowered place?**

# The Practice of Silence, Stillness & Darkness

Set aside at least twenty minutes to practice silence, stillness and darkness.

Of course, if you can do this more than once, you will receive even more benefits. But if all you can find is 10 minutes, that will still do you a world of good.

**Materials: comfortable place to lie down, eye cover/sleep mask, ear plugs or headphones if you live in a noisy environment.**

Create a warm, comfy nest with blankets and pillows. If you want to feel enclosed, build one of those blanket forts you made as a child. Make sure the room is dark and quiet.

No music, no guided meditations. Just silence, darkness and stillness for 1 hour. No problem if you fall asleep. This is not a meditation time. Try to make sure you have a "do not disturb" sign on the door, phones turned off.

Solitude is essential to creativity.

Slumber, silence, stillness and darkness are the deepest restoratives we have.

# The Nature of Suffering + Sacrifice

What flavor of suffering are you here to alleviate?

Does your ideal client experience a form of this suffering? How?

The more you tune into your SDC's suffering the more compassion you will have for them.

Where are you playing small?

Sometimes sacrificing an aspect of yourself in order to get something you want is the correct path. For example, saying "no" to fun social gatherings for 3-6 months to finish that book you've been working on for years.

Or, are you sacrificing something too precious? This can show up in many forms. Are you staying in old jobs, cluttered homes, outworn relationships or friendships because you don't want to hurt the other person, or have to change, transform, step up and be bold?

Your ideal client also sacrifices her or his happiness, success/ financial abundance and possibly even deepest soul needs to try to please others or fit into the crowd and avoid rejection.

Write down their sacrifices. Do they correlate with yours?

# Melusina's Sanctuary Meditation

The legend of the double-tailed mermaid has alchemical roots. It's a story about what happens in a watery, fluid and private sanctuary that is inviolable. A space so sacred that if it is violated, the forces of life are turned upside down.

There are different stories about Melusina, as she is known in French folklore, but all have the same plot: a hybrid woman-mermaid-serpent-dragon marries a mortal man and all is well as long as he allows her privacy each seventh day of the week while she's bathing. In her private chambers Melusine, or Melusina, reveals her true self. The taboo is potent. If she is seen in her true form the love spell is broken and she must fly away to the Other Realms leaving her mortal husband broken hearted.

This myth reveals the duality of our greatest gift—for us it is where we are most ourselves, comfortable and powerful. For others it can be frightening and intimidating. If we never reveal our true selves (the gift), we live a life of comfort and conventionality.

If we reveal our true selves we often become a target for disapproval, harsh judgment and criticism.

No wonder we hide our talents!

Still I ask you to stretch your boundaries beyond your comfort zones. Color outside the lines when you plan your offerings, marketing and branding. What the world needs is YOUR gift, in all of its unique splendor.

What are the gifts that you bring to the world now? Tend + nurture these seeds of your soul through both your livelihood and your creative projects.

**Try this short and potent visualization:**

> Close your eyes and go into a quiet, reflective state. Imagine your magical gifts floating and swirling in a cauldron large enough to fit your entire body into. Slip into this cauldron and feel yourself healed by your own gifts; the silky warm water caressing every inch of your body.
>
> Treat your gifts as they truly are. Precious. Timeless. Boundless. Each in-breath and out-breath emanates your gift's energy.
>
> Continue to feel your gifts' energies, coursing through your aura and even seeping through the membrane of your skin. Allow them to flow to your internal organs, bones and blood.
>
> It feels so delicious.

## Journaling Prompts:

What are you here on Mama Earth to give?

Why were you lovingly placed on the planet with these gifts NOW?

Take a few moments to write some stream of consciousness responses to those two questions.

# Chapter 9: SEX, POWER + MONEY

Pleasure. Passion. Permission.

*Entrepreneurship is the quest for pleasure, that only has good consequences.*

(My own moniker based on the famous Epicurus quote)

The mermaids commissioned me in 2013 to write about the importance of sexuality and sensuality and their intimate connection to business bliss and financial abundance. I hemmed and hawed.

I procrastinated for about six months.

I kept insisting to them that I didn't know what the hell to say! And they just smiled and nodded their heads.

"Yes you do. Just sit down and write."

Mermaids are wonderful guides into the realm of sexuality and sensuality, and how pleasuring ourselves is one of the most powerful acts of self-love-respect-caring.

They have been so gentle with me and simultaneously extremely persistent. I feel like a big rock of resistance being worn away by a gentle, yet neverending flow of a river.

So, yes, the mermaids finally wore me down. "Ok, I'll do it!"

Many of us are still in an interesting stage of overcoming the inhibitions and taboos around sexuality, physically experiencing + expressing pleasure. The voices in our heads still echoing the Puritanical morals that are part of the foundations of our society: sexuality and sensuality are still considered bad, ugly, evil, dirty, unclean.

It doesn't escape my awareness that we unconsciously approach money in the same shadowy way.

**Sex. Money. Power.** The complex relationship between these three areas of our lives extends into our businesses in subtle and profound ways.

I can't possibly hope to uncover all of this in one short chapter, but I hope to at least give you the inspiration to dive into this topic in revealing AND healing ways.

# What is it About Money?

You have all sorts of beliefs around money and in this section you'll dig up how you value yourself and your time in relation to the dance between you, your family, society and MONEY.

First, just begin to recall all the things you heard about money, earning and spending from your parents AND your grandparents.

If money was not discussed that often, how did your parents and grandparents act around money? Was it respected, revered, hated, feared? What were some of the emotions that money conjured up for them?

We are all called into the family + society trance at a very young and impressionable age.

**Explorations:**

Part 1. Journal about every little detail you can remember about how your parents and grandparents felt, reacted and what they believed about money. Set a timer for 30 minutes. If you stop before, that's fine. Just move forward.

The money shadow is huge for all of us, and I don't want you to get stuck. Move through quickly so the critics don't get ahold of you.

Part 2. Write down as many of your current money mantras, your beliefs around money, in 10 minutes on a piece of paper that you can burn:

- "I don't earn enough."
- "I need more money."
- "Money is the root of all evil."
- "Rich people are greedy."

Etc.

You heard me right. You are going to burn this list. You are purifying your mental, physical and spiritual space. Create a ritual to perform this week.

Suggestion: One evening in the next 4-5 days, sit outside in the dark, under a full moon if you can swing it. Look at your list one last time and say goodbye to these mantras. Burn the paper and watch the smoke rise into the darkness where these old shards are devoured by the Dark Mother, who loves us and watches over us.

Take a cleansing bath or shower to wash away last vestiges of the residue. Try adding sea salt or actual water you've collected from the ocean. As you get in the water, see the old beliefs melting and dissolving away.

Part 3. Decide on 3 or more positive or neutral new mantras you'd like to replace your old beliefs with. These can be fantastical or completely down to earth. Let your imagination take the lead. Write these down 3 times each on a piece of paper and then place them on your altar, in your journal… somewhere you'll remember to look at them.

In mentoring over 100 entrepreneurs, I'd say the biggest blocks to growth and the biggest fears are almost always around money. And how much to charge.

My business model thrives when I create offerings in price ranges to suit different economic levels. I've tried just having high-end pricing or low-end pricing or middle-of-the-road pricing. It has never worked for me. What does work for me is to have a mix of offerings starting, from free or donation-based, along with middle range and high-priced premium offerings like specialized 1:1 mentoring + implementation packages.

So, what works for you? And what doesn't?

I find the people who have the hardest time charging what they're worth are the handmade goods peeps. Be sure to figure in the actual time it takes you to make something (your "hourly" once you have your system down pat). I know, in the beginning the creative process takes time. but include your time along with the materials, shipping + tax costs.

I'm going to be a myth buster here for a moment gotta speak my truth, ya know?

It is completely untrue that if you charge more for something (service or product) that people will "show up" as their best selves or that they will not show up if it's not expensive.

People have paid me thousands of dollars and not shown up. Other people have taken my free or donation-based classes and have shown up BIG and have done the work.

It is not true that whatever you spend on biz education will net you back 10 times the amount. This is totally arbitrary! You might make more than 10 times what you spent on a course/coaching, or a lot less.

Another warning that I hear a lot is people won't respect/trust/hire you unless you have oodles of high paying clients, a huge newsletter list, thousands of Twitter followers... the list goes on. This is a huge crap pile of lies. Don't believe it. Yes, these things do help, but in the beginning, you're building up the numbers and your confidence. You are one-of-a-kind unique. You have a gift to deliver, so start delivering already!

Remember that being yourself, getting wicked-awesome at your craft, and staying the course will get you where you want to be.

Two women entrepreneurs I deeply respect are Marie Forleo and Danielle LaPorte. These women really did their work to become as successful as they are. Marie Forleo started her coaching business over 10 years ago. Her success didn't happen overnight.

Danielle LaPorte did 150 FREE 1:1 Fire Starter Sessions before charging one penny!

You know what you need to do. If you don't, ask for help.

I know that the wisdom and unique recipe for business success, on your terms, has been deep down inside you all along.

# Power

Power is a word rife with contradictions and sinister associations.

Here are a few definitions we can play with:

1.  Ability to do or act; capability of doing or accomplishing something.

2.  Political or national strength: the balance of power in Europe.

3.  Great or marked ability to do or act; strength; might; force.

4.  Control or command over others; authority; ascendancy: power over men's minds.

We want to be powerful agents of change in our own lives and be a force for positive transformation in the world at large. But so often, we are warned that power is only wielded by the evil and the greedy.

So, we turn away from it. And, by turning away, we GIVE it away.

**How will you reclaim your power?**

To me power is not about power *over someone or something*, as in domination. That is the fear-based power we are all trying to get away from.

**True power is:**

- Speaking and embodying your truth.
- Allowing your voice to be heard.
- Being visible, seen, experienced.
- Making your own decisions and living by them.
- Empowering others by holding that they too are powerful, no matter what the outer circumstances look like.

*What else would you add to this list?*

Expressing yourself authentically is powerful. It will draw masses of people to you, people who are moved by your story.

Who knows, you may save a life, a marriage or give hope to someone who is ready to give up.

Now, that's immense power!

**Bonus**

Use my guided visualization to build your personal power and connect it with Divine Will:

> Chakra Triad Meditation/Breathing. Links Heart, Sacral and Root Chakras (www.amazon.com/clouddrive/share?s=JYxnk1D_QJwlD0NqChkFps)

# Chapter 10: Shapeshifter

The shapeshifter is one of my favorite archetypes. We tend to make this archetype more shallow than it actually is. Part of that is how we talk about archetypes in contemporary time.

In general, I find that "archetype" has become a catch word. It sounds interesting, but people either don't want to dig deeply into it or they don't know how to. I'm going to give you an overview of Shapeshifter that is a lot more mythic and archetypal.

An archetype is an invisible pattern, like a blueprint of behaviors and how they function within our personality. The idea comes mostly from psychology, particularly Jungian psychology. Later James Hillman expanded and deepened Jungian Psychology into what we call Archetypal Psychology.

To most people today, a *shapeshifter* is somebody who changes their image frequently; sometimes simple style changes such as hairstyle or hair color. Madonna is a great example from the 90s. Lady Gaga is the shapeshifter of present; most pop stars have the capability of showing different aspects of their persona. Even though we sometimes call them shapeshifters (looking at them from a more superficial perspective), they are not *really* shapeshifters in the archetypal sense.

We need to dig deeper.

The Shapeshifter acts as a catalyst for change. It's a symbol of the psychological need for transformation.

Shapeshifter is the most dynamic and unstable of all the archetypes. It's nearly impossible to pin one down. Similar to Trickster, Shapeshifter seeks to conceal or hide something. I'll use some classic myths to explain how this works. The shapeshifter, particularly in stories and myths, expresses the energy of the animus, which is the male element in female consciousness. The anima is the female element in the male consciousness. Many shapeshifters appear as the hero's lover. Every now and then the hero is the shapeshifter in the story.

One of the most common shapeshifter types is the *femme fatale*— a woman who seduces and destroys. One example is Glenn Close in *Fatal Attraction,* who appears as a beautiful sensual Aphrodite woman but inside she's this crazy murderous monster. Other shapeshifters would be werewolves or the Selkie, (mer creatures that appear as seals until they remove their skins and reveal their womanly forms).

This transformational aspect is dazzling but also confusing because you don't know which one is real: the wolf or man, the seal or the woman. In the movie *Basic Instinct* with Sharon Stone... just before the end you think "Yeah, she's this beautiful woman. We just didn't want to trust her." But... at the end she's making love and you see the infamous ice pick under the bed. You are left with a strong element of doubt. The shapeshifter always makes you think twice about whether or not you can completely trust him or her.

As an entrepreneur, when I reveal something about myself, I do it hoping my clients will feel like they know me better and can trust me more. But sometimes someone will reveal something that makes me think, "If they are revealing that, I wonder what are they concealing?" That's true for all of us. We're not always conscious of what we're concealing. We are dealing here with the realm of the unconscious. We only recognize what we've been concealing when it comes into consciousness. And that can get into the shadow. Shapeshifter is not the shadow but it teases us into that realm a bit.

A classic shapeshifter would be the sea god Proteus in the Odyssey. On their way back from the Trojan War, Menelaus and his men go to an island where they have to capture Proteus to find out how to return home to Ithaca. The problem is that Proteus is, well, *"protean."* We often say shapeshifters are protean, referring to the god Proteus. (He's also called the Old Man of the Sea.) To get him to tell you the truth, you have to hold onto him as he changes form.

If you let go, he won't divulge the truth. So Menelaus and his men hold onto Proteus for dear life as he turns into a lion, a volcano, and all these different forms.

The lesson is: if you can be patient with the shapeshifter and hold on, the truth will be revealed. But the shapeshifter will show all its different faces to hide the truth.

Journaling questions:

- Who am I today?

- Who do I wish I was?

- Why does this appeal to me?

Use a timer and give yourself two minutes for each of the questions, or maybe six or seven minutes for all three. Having the shorter span of time to do it turns off your inner critic and helps you keep writing, no matter what comes out. Don't lift your pen or pencil off the page. Do a complete flow-of-consciousness dump onto your paper or computer.

A second inquiry will take you a level deeper.

Look at "Who am I today" and "Who do I wish I was" to see if there is a big difference between the two. That could indicate some transformations you need to make in your life to become this person, what you really want.

**By being this person, I am revealing... (Spend two or three minutes on this.)**

**By being this person, I am concealing...**

**(This will be a little more difficult because you're digging into the shadow side of Shapeshifter, which does not want to be seen. Give yourself eight to ten minutes to do this inquiry.)**

# Resources + Bibliography

Babauta, Leo. "The Practice of Work Mind & Vacation Mind, Simultaneously" http://zenhabits.net/zenwork.

Bradley, Marion Zimmer. *The Mists of Avalon*. Ballantine Books, 1987.

Campbell, Joseph. *Myths of Light: Eastern Metaphors of the Eternal*. New World Library, 2012.

—. *The Hero With a Thousand Faces*. 3rd printing. Princeton, New Jersey: Princeton UP, 1973.

—. *An Open Life: Joseph Campbell in Conversation With Michael Toms*. Ed. John M. Maher and Dennie Briggs. Burdett, New York: New Dimensions Foundation, 1988.

Chuen, Lam Kam. *The Feng Shui Handbook: How To Create A Healthier Living & Working Environment*. Holt Paperbacks, 1996.

Coelho, Paulo. *The Alchemist*. 10th Anniversary Edition. Harper San Francisco, 1998.

Corbin, Henry. "Mundus Imaginalis or The Imaginary and the Imaginal." Paper. Spring 1972 - Zürich.

Estes, Clarissa Pinkola. *Women Who Run With the Wolves: Myths and Stories of the Wild Woman Archetype*. Mass Market Paperback, 1996.

Hillman, James. *Archetypal Psychology*. 3rd ed. Putnam, Connecticut: Spring Publications, 2004.

—. *A Blue Fire: Selected Writings by James Hillman*. Ed. Thomas Moore. New York: Harper Collins, 1991.

—. "An Inquiry into Image." *Spring* (1977): 62-88.

—. Lecture to the National Congress of Jungian Analysts, Boston, MA, Oct. 1993.

—. *Re-Visioning Psychology*. New York: Harper, 1992.

—. *The Thought of the Heart and the Soul of the World*. Dallas: Spring, 1993.

Jung, Carl G. *The Collected Works of C. G. Jung*. Ed. and trans. Gerhard Adler and R. F. C. Hull. Vol. 6. Princeton: Princeton UP, 1971.

—. *The Collected Works of C. G. Jung*. Ed. and trans. Gerhard Adler and R. F. C. Hull. Vol. 7. 2nd ed. Princeton: Princeton UP, 1966.

—. *The Collected Works of C. G. Jung*. Ed. and trans. Gerhard Adler and R. F. C. Hull. Vol. 8. 2nd ed. Princeton: Princeton UP, 1969.

—. *The Collected Works of C. G. Jung*. Ed. and trans. Gerhard Adler and R. F. C. Hull. Vol. 9i. Princeton: Princeton UP. 1959.

—. *The Collected Works of C. G. Jung*. Ed. and trans. Gerhard Adler and R. F. C. Hull. Vol. 9ii. 2nd ed. Princeton: Princeton UP. 1959.

—. *The Collected Works of C. G. Jung*. Ed. and trans. Gerhard Adler and R. F. C. Hull. Vol. 11. 2nd ed. Princeton: Princeton UP, 1969.

—. *The Collected Works of C. G. Jung*. Ed. and trans. Gerhard Adler and R. F. C. Hull. Vol. 12. 2nd ed. Princeton: Princeton UP, 1968.

—. *The Collected Works of C. G. Jung*. Ed. and trans. Gerhard Adler and R. F. C. Hull. Vol. 13. Princeton: Princeton UP, 1967.

—. *The Collected Works of C. G. Jung*. Ed. and trans. Gerhard Adler and R. F. C. Hull. Vol. 14. 2nd ed. Princeton: Princeton UP, 1970.

—. *The Collected Works of C. G. Jung*. Ed. and trans. Gerhard Adler and R. F. C. Hull. Vol. 17. Princeton: Princeton UP, 1954.

—. *The Collected Works of C. G. Jung*. Ed. and trans. Gerhard Adler and R. F. C. Hull. Vol. 18. Princeton: Princeton UP. 1976.

—. *Psychology and Religion*. New Haven: Yale UP, 1938.

—. *Four Archetypes*. Trans. R. F. C. Hull. Princeton, New Jersey: Princeton UP, 1973.

*Orixás da Bahia*. Dir. Lazaro Faria. Casa de Cinema da Bahia, 2005. DVD.

Ragan, Kathleen. *Fearless Girls, Wise Women & Beloved Sisters: Heroines in Folktales from Around the World*. New York, London: W.W. Norton & Company, 1998.

Rebelle Society. www.rebellesociety.com.

Slattery, Dennis. *The Wounded Body: Remembering the Markings of Flesh*. SUNY, 1999.

Tannen, Ricki Stefanie. *The Female Trickster: The Mask That Reveals. Post-Jungian and Postmodern Psychological Perspectives on Women in Contemporary Culture*. London: Routledge, 2007.

Tipton, James. "Eating the World." www.coloradopoetscenter. org/poets/tipton_james/eating.html

Turner, Victor. *The Anthropology of Performance*. New York: PAJ, 1988.

—. *Dramas, Fields and Metaphors: Symbolic Action in Human Society*. Ithaca: Cornell UP, 1974.

—. *The Ritual Process: Structure and Anti-Structure*. Ithaca: Cornell UP, 1969.

Vogler, Christopher. *The Writer's Journey: Mythic Structure for Writers*. Third Edition. Michael Wiese Productions, 2007.

Woodman, Marion. *Addiction to Perfection: The Still Unravished Bride*. Toronto, Canada: Inner City Books, 1982.

—. *The Pregnant Virgin: A Process of Psychological Transformation*. Toronto, Canada: Inner City Books, 1985.

# More Resources

*I have personally experienced and highly recommend the following individuals and small businesses…*

## Chakra Books

Anodea, Judith, Ph.D. *Wheels of Life: The Classic Guide to the Chakra System, 2nd Edition.* Llewellyn Publications, 2013.

Judith, Anodea and Selene Vega. *The Sevenfold Journey: Reclaiming Mind, Body & Spirit Through the Chakras.* Crossing Press, 1993.

## Branding

**Kris Oster, Ph.D**
Mythic Rhythm
www.krisoster.com

**Aliza Stein**
A Freaking Great Company
www.afreakinggreatcompany.com

## Astro-Biz/Tarot Readers + Intuitive Coaches

**Amethyst Mahoney, Ph.D**
www.amethystmahoney.com

**Theresa Reed**
The Tarot Lady
www.thetarotlady.com

**Safron Rossi, Ph.D**
The Archetypal Eye, Astrology
www.thearchetypaleye.com

**Tara Villeneuve**
Cosmic Soul Medicine
www.cosmicsoulmedicine.com

## Coaches

**S. M. Boyce**
Author of the popular Grimoire Series
www.writing.smboyce.com

**Cindie Chavez**
Love + Magic Coach
www.cindiechavez.com

**Rheba Estante**
Drafting Your First Book Coach
www.voiceitwrite30daysbook.squarespace.com

**Tanja Gardner**
Conscious Introvert Success
www.consciousintrovertsuccess.com

**Tanya Geisler**
www.tanyageisler.com

**Sarah Hawkins**
Sacred Comfort
www.sacredcomfort.com

**Helen Hodgson**
Serve The Goddess Mobile Spa, Goddess Retreats, Coach
www.servethegoddess.com
www.howtocreateamobilespabusiness.com

**Karey Pohn, Ph.D**
www.personaleverestcoaching.com

**Dyana Valentine**
www.dyanavalentine.com

**Michelle Ward**
When I Grow Up Coach
www.whenigrowupcoach.com

## Strategists

**Halley Grey**
Evolve + Succeed
www.evolveandsucceed.com

**Angie Mrockza**
*(Angie was the strategist and launch manager for this book!)*
www.angiemroczka.com

**Aliza Stein**
A Freaking Great Company
www.afreakinggreatcompany.com

## Copywriters/Editors

**Chrissy Dass**
www.chrissydas.com

**Tanja Gardner**
Crystal Clarity Copywriting
www.crystalclaritycopywriting.com

**Kris Oster, Ph.D**
Mythic Rhythm
www.krisoster.com

**Nancy Oster**
*(editor of this book, oh yeah!)*
www.nancyoster.com

## Marketing/PR

**Melissa Cassera**
www.melissacassera.com

**Marie Forleo**
www.marieforleo.com

**Alexandra Franzen**
www.alexandrafranzen.com

**Halley Grey**
Evolve + Succeed
www.evolveandsucceed.com

**Susan Harrow**
www.susanharrow.com

**Danielle LaPorte**
www.daniellelaporte.com

**Angie Mrockza**
www.angiemroczka.com

**Danielle Seraphine**
MAM : Marketing Automation Mavens Certified Ontraport
Consultant
www.marketingautomationmavens.com

## Artists/Illustrators/Designers

**Sarah Leonard**
Curiously Sarah, A Cat-Like Curiosity
www.curiouslysarah.com

**Demi Mermaid Priestess**
www.priestesstraining.com

**Angie Mrockza**
www.angiemroczka.com

**Kent Youngstrom**
www.kentyoungstrom.com

## Photographers

**Catherine Just**
www.catherinejust.com

**Jill Martin**
Kind Eyes Photography
www.kindeyes.com

**Rachel Sarah Thurston**
www.rsthurston.blogspot.com

**Monica True**
www.monicatrue.com

## Music/Composition

**Shaun Oster**
www.doubleheadmusic.com

## Web Developers

**Nikole Gipps**
That Super Girl!
www.thatsupergirl.com

**Christine Leiser Consulting**
www.christineleiser.com

**Angie Mrockza**
www.angiemroczka.com

**Shaun Oster**
www.doubleheadmusic.com

## Online Communities

**Aspiring SuperNova Tribe for Purpose-Centered Entrepreneurs Facebook Group** (free)
led by Lena Ski
www.facebook.com/groups/SuperNovaSessions

**Authentic Connecting Facebook Group** (free)
led by Jodi Chapman
www.facebook.com/groups/authenticconnecting/

**Conscious Introvert Awesomeness Facebook Group** (free)
led by Tanja Gardner
www.facebook.com/groups/310914615738736

**Curious Artists Community Facebook Group** (free)
led by Sarah Leonard
www.facebook.com/groups/thecuriousartistscommunity

**Dream Career Creators Facebook Group** (free)
led by Michelle Ward
www.facebook.com/groups/1524720564411582

**Evolve's Internet Domination Club Facebook Group** (free)
led by Halley Gray
www.facebook.com/groups/evolvesucceed

**The Haven** (paid membership group)
led by Author S.M. Boyce
http://smboyce.com/boyces-tribe

**Karen Tate**
Author, Goddess Advocate, Speaker, Sacred Tour Director,
Radio Show Hostess
www.karentate.com

**Spiritual Badass Facebook Group** (free)
led by Amethyst Mahoney
www.facebook.com/groups/SpiritualBadass

**The Writers' Alliance Facebook Group** (free)
led by Angie Mroczka
www.facebook.com/groups/ebookalliance

**Enchanted Entrepreneurs Circle Facebook Group** (free)
To join the group, send an email to the author and friend her
on Facebook: Kris Oster, Ph.D (eec@mythicrhythm.com)

# Acknowledgements

This book that you hold in your hands was originally delivered as two branding and business design playshops in 2013-2014: *Return to Enchantment* and *Bewitch*.

In March of 2014 I was invited to participate in a pilot mastermind group for new non-fiction authors entitled *Voice it Write: 30 Days to a Book*, led by the talented and tenacious Rheba Estante. I wrote an extremely rough draft of the first seven chapters in 30 days!

It took me a full year of rewrites to produce the version you now hold in your hands. Rheba, your loving and insightful guidance made this book happen. Thank you for believing in me.

Another person who is responsible for the beautiful look and feel of this book and its companion website is Angie Mroczka. Angie designed the compelling cover and formatted it all for digital and print… and built the website… and helped manage my blog tour. I can't recommend this woman enough. She transported me from first time author to thriving writer. I bow to you Angie!

My beta readers Cindie Chavez and Karuna Glumb were the first to see the rough draft, Lord have mercy! What a mess it was! Yet their wise and thoughtful feedback was given with the deepest love + compassion. Thank you ladies!

Huge thanks to all of my Indiegogo funders… and special nods to my biggest supporters on the campaign: Tamara Rosenberg, Nancy Norbeck, Charlotte Cressey, Karey Pohn, Maddy Vertenten, Aliza Stein and Garrett Squires.

I had over 100 wonderful + willing guinea pigs work with this material and help me to refine it. Here are just a few off of the top of my head: Maria Bovin deLabbe, Meegan Care, Pamela Chen, Chris Doggett, Merry Wise, Kim Tennant, Lyn Thurman, Cathie

Rayes, Carolina Horning, Sarah Martin Hawkins, Karin Robbins, Janet Callahan, Rose Reed (aka Mom), Aparna Khanolkar, Sandi Davis, and Tanja Gardner.

Thank you for trusting me with your inner lives and helping me to become a better teacher.

# About the Author

**Kris Oster** loves defying convention and is satisfied to be anything but 'normal.'

She was a rock star marketing director and lead website developer for some pretty big names, including Citrix Online, E! Entertainment Television, Disney, ABC, Paramount Pictures. She even made her employer $1 million with a single e-newsletter once.

But, like you, she heard the siren's call and decided to pursue a life of satisfaction, doing what she loves.

In her business and on her blog, Mythic Rhythm, Kris inspires entrepreneurs who are determine to find more meaning in their business. Through coaching and consultations with heart-centered business owners, she helps them to uncover their own uniqueness and reveal their personal mythology.

When Kris isn't working, you can find her basking along the California coastline, playing her congas, going on dates with her sexy husband, playing in the surf with her 6-year old girl, or talking to Mer-Angels.

Visit her online and view her expansive list of offerings at www. mythicrhythm.com.

**Visit the book website and enter your name and email address to get the companion audio meditations, bonus material and worksheets at: www.returntoenchantment.com**